James V Stone, Honorary Associate Professor, University of Sheffield, UK.

Information Theory
in 80 Pages

James V Stone

Title: Information Theory in 80 Pages
Author: James V Stone

©2023 Sebtel Press

First Edition, 2023.
Typeset in LaTeX 2_ε.
First printing.

ISBN 9781739672782

Cover image Claude Shannon (1916–2001). Courtesy MIT Museum.

The founding fathers of the modern computer age – Alan Turing, John von Neumann, Claude Shannon – all understood the central importance of information theory, and today we have come to realise that almost everything can either be thought of or expressed in this paradigm. I believe that, one day, information will come to be viewed as being as fundamental as energy and matter.

Demis Hassabis (CEO and co-founder of DeepMind), 2017.

Contents

Preface

1. **The Laws of Information**   1

2. **Defining Information, Bit by Bit**   3
   2.1. Decisions, Decisions 3
   2.2. Bits Are Not Binary Digits 5
   2.3. Surprisal 5
   2.4. Shannon's Desiderata 7

3. **Entropy of Discrete Variables**   9
   3.1. Flipping a Coin 10
   3.2. Dicing with Entropy 12
   3.3. Interpreting Entropy 14

4. **Entropy of Continuous Variables**   17
   4.1. The Trouble with Entropy 17
   4.2. Differential Entropy 20
   4.3. What is Half a Bit of Information? 20

5. **Maximum Entropy Distributions**   23
   5.1. Why Maximum Entropy? 23
   5.2. The Uniform Distribution 23
   5.3. The Exponential Distribution 25
   5.4. The Gaussian Distribution 26

6. **Noiseless Channels**   29
   6.1. The Source Coding Theorem 29
   6.2. Why the Theorem is True 32
   6.3. A Picture of Information 34

7. Mutual Information and Noise   **39**

  7.1. Noise 39

  7.2. Joint Entropy 42

  7.3. Mutual Information for Discrete Variables 42

  7.4. Mutual Information for Continuous variables 44

  7.5. Mutual Information and Joint Entropy 45

8. Noisy Channels   **47**

  8.1. The Noisy Channel Coding Theorem 47

  8.2. Why the Theorem is True 48

  8.3. The Gaussian Channel 49

9. Rate Distortion Theory   **51**

  9.1. Rate Distortion Theory 52

  9.2. The Binary Rate Distortion Function 54

  9.3. The Gaussian Rate Distortion Function 55

  9.4. Image Compression Example 56

10. Transfer Entropy   **61**

  10.1. Transfer Entropy 61

  10.2. The Pendulum 64

  10.3. Numerical Example 65

Further Reading   **67**

Appendices

A. Glossary   **69**

B. Key Equations   **73**

References   **75**

Index   **79**

Preface

Who Needs a Short Book?

This short book is a primer for students and researchers who wish to gain a firm grasp of the basics of information theory without extensive explanatory text. Despite its brevity, this book retains the informal writing style to be found in the more loquacious books within this Tutorial Introduction series.

As Mark Twain famously said, "I didn't have time to write a short letter, so I wrote a long one instead." By way of analogy, it is relatively easy to write a long book, which follows every tangential whim of thought along a circuitous route to a handful of rarefied facts perched on some distant horizon. But writing a short book, which discards all but the most essential facts and distills them into a coherent account, is much, much harder (involving removal of much, much repetition). So here it is – the essence of information theory in 80 pages.

Who Should Read This Book?

The material in this book should be accessible to anyone with an understanding of basic mathematics. The tutorial style adopted ensures that readers who are prepared to put in the effort will be rewarded with a solid grasp of the fundamentals of information theory.

Matlab and Python Computer Code

It often aids understanding to be able to examine well-documented computer code that provides an example of a particular calculation or method. To support this, Matlab and Python code implementing key information-theoretic methods, and which also reproduces some of the figures in this book, can be downloaded from here:
https://jamesstone.sites.sheffield.ac.uk/books/infoshort

Corrections

Please email corrections to j.v.stone@sheffield.ac.uk.

A list of corrections can be found at

`https://jamesstone.sites.sheffield.ac.uk/books/infoshort`

Acknowledgements

Thanks to Alice Yew for meticulous copy-editing and proofreading. For permission to use the photograph of Claude Shannon, thanks to the Massachusetts Institute of Technology.

Jim Stone, Sheffield, England, 2022.

Chapter 1

The Laws of Information

The universe is conventionally described in terms of physical quantities such as mass and velocity, but a quantity at least as important as these is *information*. Whether we consider computers[18], evolution[2;11], physics[8], black holes[15], artificial intelligence[4], quantum computation[32] or the brain[10;29], we are driven inexorably to the conclusion that the behaviour of these systems is determined mainly by the way they process information.

In 1948, Claude Shannon published a paper called *A Mathematical Theory of Communication*[33]. This paper heralded a transformation in our understanding of information. Before Shannon's paper, information had been viewed as a kind of poorly defined miasmic fluid. But after Shannon's paper, it became apparent that information is a well-defined and, above all, *measurable* quantity.

Information theory is defined in terms of a few key *mathematical theorems* (a theorem is just a mathematical statement that has been proven to be true). This revolutionary theory underpins so many applications and fields of research that its theorems deserve to be called the *laws of information*.

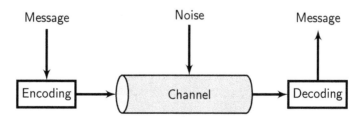

Figure 1.1: The communication channel. A message (data) is encoded before being used as input to a communication channel, which adds noise. The channel output is decoded by a receiver to recover the message.

The Laws of Information

To set the scene for a brief overview, consider Figure 1.1 in the following context (the technical terms used below are explained in later chapters).

A *source* (e.g. a theatre stage) generates *messages* (e.g. lines spoken by actors) with a fixed amount of information per second. These messages are recorded (e.g. by a TV camera) before being *encoded* by a computer and then used as input to a *communication channel* (e.g. a satellite). The maximum rate at which information can be *transmitted* through this channel is its *channel capacity*. The channel can be subject to the effects of random *noise*, which corrupts the encoded message to some extent and thus reduces the capacity of the channel. Finally, the channel output is *decoded* (e.g. by a TV), which can then yield either

a) the original message if the information rate from the source is less than the channel capacity, or

b) an approximation to the original message if the information rate from the source is larger than the channel capacity.

Now the laws of information can be summarised as follows:

1. The *source coding theorem* states that there exists an encoding of messages which allows them to be transmitted at a rate arbitrarily close to the channel capacity (see Chapter 6).

2. The *noisy channel coding theorem* specifies the extent to which noise reduces channel capacity, and states that there exists an encoding of messages which allows them to be transmitted at a rate arbitrarily close to this reduced capacity (see Chapter 8).

3. The *rate distortion theorem* states that if the amount of information in the messages exceeds the channel capacity then channel output values can still be used to estimate input values, but the uncertainty in those estimates cannot be less than the difference between the amount of information in the messages and the channel capacity (see Chapter 9).

Chapter 2

Defining Information, Bit by Bit

2.1. Decisions, Decisions

Information is usually measured in *bits*, where one bit is the amount of information required to choose between two equally probable, or *equiprobable*, alternatives.

Imagine you are standing at the fork in the road at point A in Figure 2.1 and you want to get to the point marked D. The fork at A represents two equiprobable alternatives, so if I instruct you to go left then you have received one bit of information. If we represent my instruction with a *binary digit* (0 = left and 1 = right) then this binary digit provides you with one bit of information, which tells you which road to choose.

> **Key point.** A *bit* is the amount of information required to choose between two equiprobable alternatives.

Now imagine that you come to another fork, at point B. Again, a binary digit (1 = right) provides one bit of information, allowing you to choose the correct road, which leads to C. Note that C is one of four possible interim destinations that you could have reached from A after making two decisions. The two binary digits that allow you to make the correct decisions provided two bits of information, enabling you to choose from four equiprobable alternatives; 4 equals $2 \times 2 = 2^2$.

A third binary digit (1 = right) provides you with one more bit of information, which allows you to again choose the correct road, leading to the point marked D. There are now eight paths you could have chosen from starting at A, so three binary digits (which provide you with three bits of information) allow you to choose from eight equiprobable alternatives; 8 equals $2 \times 2 \times 2 = 2^3$.

We can restate this in more general terms if we use n to represent the number of forks and m to represent the number of final destinations. If you have passed n forks then you have effectively chosen from $m = 2^n$ destinations. Because the decision at each fork requires one bit of information, n forks require n bits of information.

Viewed from another perspective, if there are $m = 8$ possible destinations then the number of forks is $n = 3$, which is the *logarithm* of 8. Thus, $3 = \log_2 8$ is the number of forks implied by eight destinations. More generally, the logarithm of m is the power to which 2 must be raised in order to obtain m; that is, $2^n = m$. This relationship can be expressed in terms of a logarithm as $n = \log_2 m$. The subscript 2 indicates that we are using logarithms to the base 2. All logarithms in this book use base 2 unless stated otherwise.

If we double the number of destinations to $2m$, the number of bits we would need to make decisions at the forks is

$$\log(2m) = \log m + \log 2 \tag{2.1}$$
$$= n + 1 \text{ bits.} \tag{2.2}$$

So, if n forks imply $m = 2^n$ alternative destinations then $n + 1$ forks imply $2^{n+1} = 2^n \times 2 = 2m$ alternative destinations. In other words, if we need n bits of information to navigate to one out of m equiprobable destinations then we need $n + 1$ bits to navigate to one out of $2m$ equiprobable destinations.

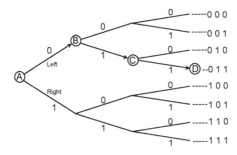

Figure 2.1: For a traveller who does not know the way, making a correct decision at each fork in the road requires one bit of information. The 0s and 1s on the right-hand side summarise the instructions needed to arrive at each destination; a left turn is indicated by a 0 and a right turn by a 1.

> **Key point.** If you have n bits of information then you can choose from $m = 2^n$ equiprobable alternatives. Equivalently, if you have to choose between m equiprobable alternatives then you need $n = \log_2 m$ bits of information. If you have to choose between $2m$ equiprobable alternatives then you need $n+1$ bits.

2.2. Bits Are Not Binary Digits

The word *bit* is a portmanteau, derived by combining the first part of *binary* with the final part of *digit*. However, a bit and a binary digit are fundamentally different types of quantities. A binary digit is the value of a binary variable, where this value can only be a 0 or a 1.

In contrast, a bit is an *amount of information*, and the number of bits conveyed by a binary digit can vary between 0 and 1. In the example above, the amount of information conveyed by each binary digit was chosen to be exactly 1 bit, but that is not always the case, as we shall see below. By analogy, just as a pint bottle can carry between zero and one pint of liquid, so a binary digit can convey between zero and one bit of information.

> **Key point.** A bit is the *amount of information* required to choose between two equiprobable alternatives (e.g. left/right), whereas a binary digit is the *value of a binary variable*, which can adopt one of two possible values (i.e. 0 or 1).

2.3. Surprisal

Just as there were 2 equiprobable outcomes at each fork in the road in the example above, so there are 2 equiprobable outcomes when a coin is flipped. And just as 1 bit is required to choose the correct road from the 2 alternatives at each fork, so 1 bit is required to predict which of 2 equiprobable outcomes will be obtained from a single coin flip. Conversely, observing the outcome of a single coin flip with 2 equiprobable outcomes provides 1 bit, whether the outcome is a head x_h or a tail x_t.

The amount of information associated with a single event is called the *surprisal*, represented with a lower-case h here. The surprisal of each of m equiprobable outcomes is defined as the logarithm of m:

$$h \quad = \quad \log m \text{ bits.} \tag{2.3}$$

For example, the surprisal of a head x_h and of a tail x_t is

$$h(x_h) = \log m = \log 2 = 1 \text{ bit,} \tag{2.4}$$
$$h(x_t) = \log m = \log 2 = 1 \text{ bit.} \tag{2.5}$$

We can adopt a different perspective, which seems almost trivial in the case of a fair coin but yields insight for unfair coins, as we shall see. For a fair coin, the probability of a head is $p(x_h) = 1/m = 0.5$, so $m = 1/p(x_h)$ and the amount of information obtained when a head is observed is given by its surprisal

$$h(x_h) = \log 1/p(x_h) = \log 1/0.5 = 1 \text{ bit;} \tag{2.6}$$

similarly, the surprisal of a tail is $h(x_t) = \log 1/p(x_t) = 1$ bit.

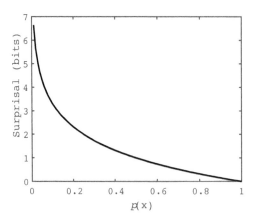

Figure 2.2: Shannon information as surprisal. Values of x that are less probable have larger values of surprisal, $h(x) = \log_2 1/p(x)$ bits.

Now consider an unfair coin that lands heads up 90% of the time. When this coin is flipped, we expect it to land heads up, so when it does so we are less surprised than when it lands tails up. The more improbable a particular outcome is, the more surprised we will be to observe it. In this case, the surprisal of a head is (see Figure 2.2)

$$h(x_h) \quad = \quad \log 1/p(x_h) \text{ bits} \tag{2.7}$$
$$= \quad -\log p(x_h) \text{ bits.} \tag{2.8}$$

With $p(x_h) = 0.9$, the surprisal of a head comes to a mere $h(x_h) = 0.15$ bits, while the surprisal of a tail is $h(x_h) = \log 1/p(x_t) = \log 1/0.1 = 3.32$ bits (we shall return to this example later). The Shannon information of an outcome is defined as its surprisal, so more improbable outcomes provide greater amounts of information.

> **Key Point.** Shannon information is a measure of surprise. The amount of information, or surprisal, of an outcome x that occurs with probability $p(x)$ is $h(x) = \log 1/p(x)$.

2.4. Shannon's Desiderata

Shannon stated that any logically consistent mathematical definition of information has to satisfy a particular set of conditions.

1. **Additivity.** The total amount of information of a set of individual outcomes (e.g. coin flips) is obtained by *adding* the information of those outcomes.
2. **Continuity.** The information of an outcome (e.g. obtaining a head from a coin flip) increases continuously (i.e. smoothly) as the probability of that outcome decreases.
3. **Symmetry.** The information of a sequence of outcomes is the same irrespective of the order in which those outcomes occur.

Crucially, Shannon[35] proved that the definition of information given in the Key Point above is the only one which meets all of these conditions.

Chapter 3

Entropy of Discrete Variables

We can represent each outcome as the value of a random variable X. In practice, we are not usually interested in the surprisal of a particular value of a random variable, but rather in how much surprisal, on *average*, is associated with the entire set of possible values that the variable can adopt. The average surprisal of a random variable X is called its *Shannon entropy* or *entropy*.

The entropy of an independent and identically distributed (iid) random variable X is defined in terms of its *probability distribution* $p(X)$ (all variables are assumed to be iid unless stated otherwise). Given a discrete random variable $X = \{x_1, x_2, \ldots, x_N\}$ with a probability distribution $p(X) = \{p(x_1), p(x_2), \ldots, p(x_N)\}$, its entropy is defined as the average surprisal

$$H(X) \quad = \quad \sum_{i=1}^{N} p(x_i)\, h(x_i) \qquad\qquad (3.1)$$

$$= \quad \sum_{i=1}^{N} p(x_i) \log \frac{1}{p(x_i)} \qquad\qquad (3.2)$$

$$= \quad \mathrm{E}[\log 1/p(x_i)] \text{ bits,} \qquad\qquad (3.3)$$

where $\mathrm{E}[\,\cdot\,]$ represents the *expected value* of the quantity in square brackets. Shannon's *source coding theorem* (Chapter 6) guarantees that, to a first approximation, each value of the variable X can be represented with an average of $H(X)$ binary digits.

> **Key Point.** The entropy of a random variable is the average surprisal over all possible values of that variable.

3.1. Flipping a Coin

The Entropy of a Fair Coin

The average surprisal associated with a coin flip can be found as follows. If the coin is fair or unbiased then $p(x_h) = p(x_t) = 0.5$, so the Shannon information gained when either a head or a tail is observed is the surprisal $\log 1/0.5 = 1$ bit (using Equation 2.6). Since the surprisal of a head and the surprisal of a tail are both equal to 1 bit, the average Shannon information gained after a coin flip is also 1 bit. Because entropy is defined as average surprisal, it follows that the entropy of a fair coin is $H(X) = 1$ bit.

The Entropy of an Unfair Coin

Suppose a coin is biased such that the probability of a head is $p(x_h) = 0.9$; then it is easy to predict the result of each coin flip (i.e. with 90% accuracy if we predict a head for each flip). If the outcome is a head then the amount of Shannon information gained is

$$h(x_h) \quad = \quad \log 1/0.9 \qquad\qquad (3.4)$$
$$= \quad 0.15 \text{ bits.} \qquad\qquad (3.5)$$

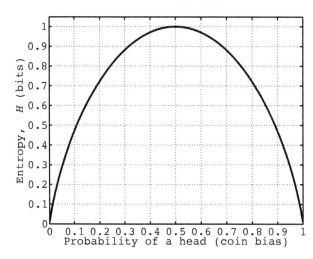

Figure 3.1: Graph of entropy $H(X)$ versus coin bias (probability $p(x_h)$ of a head). Entropy is the average amount of surprisal or Shannon information of the distribution of possible outcomes (i.e. heads and tails).

But if the outcome is a tail then the Shannon information gained is

$$h(x_t) \quad = \quad \log 1/0.1 \qquad\qquad (3.6)$$

$$= \quad 3.32 \text{ bits.} \qquad\qquad (3.7)$$

Notice that more information is gained from more surprising outcomes.

Key Point. The more improbable or surprising an outcome is, the more information it provides.

Since the proportion of flips that yield a head is $p(x_h)$ and the proportion of flips that yield a tail is $p(x_t)$ (where $p(x_h) + p(x_t) = 1$), the entropy (average surprisal) is

$$H(X) \quad = \quad p(x_h) \log \frac{1}{p(x_h)} + p(x_t) \log \frac{1}{p(x_t)} \qquad\qquad (3.8)$$

$$= \quad 0.9 \times 0.15 + 0.1 \times 3.32 \quad = \quad 0.47 \text{ bits}, \qquad (3.9)$$

as in Figure 3.1. Denoting a tail by $x_1 = x_t$ and a head by $x_2 = x_h$, we can rewrite Equation 3.8 in the form of Equation 3.3 with $N = 2$:

$$H(X) \quad = \quad \sum_{i=1}^{2} p(x_i) \log \frac{1}{p(x_i)} \text{ bits.} \qquad\qquad (3.10)$$

A Note on Nomenclature

The terms surprisal, information and Shannon entropy are often used interchangeably in the literature on information theory. Indeed, they are occasionally used interchangeably in this text, where the intended meaning is fairly obvious from the context, as explained in Section 3.3. Incidentally, the term Shannon entropy is often used to differentiate it from the term entropy used in physics [37].

3.2. Dicing with Entropy

The Entropy of an 8-Sided Die

From this point on, it will prove useful to distinguish between an *outcome* and its value, or the *outcome value* associated with that outcome. Throwing an 8-sided die (Figure 3.2a) yields an outcome. If we define the outcome value as the number on the upper face then there are $N = 8$ possible outcome values, $A_x = \{1, 2, 3, 4, 5, 6, 7, 8\}$, which can be represented by the symbols $x_1, \ldots, x_8$. For a fair die, all 8 outcomes are equally probable, so the probability of each outcome value is $p(x_i) = 1/8$.

These 8 probabilities can be represented as the probability distribution $p(X) = \{p(x_1), \ldots, p(x_8)\}$ shown in Figure 3.2b. Using Equation 3.3, the entropy of this distribution is

$$H(X) = \sum_{i=1}^{8} p(x_i) \log \frac{1}{p(x_i)}, \tag{3.11}$$

where $\log 1/p(x_i) = \log 1/(1/8) = \log 8 = 3$, so that

$$H(X) = \sum_{i=1}^{8} \frac{1}{8} \times 3 \tag{3.12}$$

$$= 3 \text{ bits.} \tag{3.13}$$

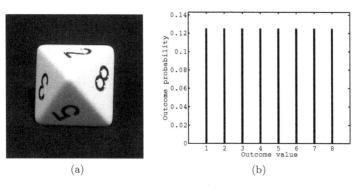

(a) (b)

Figure 3.2: (a) An 8-sided die. (b) The probability distribution of outcomes is uniform and has an entropy of $\log 8 = 3$ bits.

In words, each die outcome provides 3 bits of information. Because the entropy is the average information provided by each outcome, and because in this case each outcome provides the same amount of information, the entropy of a fair 8-sided die is also 3 bits.

The Entropy of a 6-Sided Die

Throwing a 6-sided die yields an outcome. If we define the outcome value as the number on the upper face then there are $N = 6$ possible outcome values, $A_x = \{1, 2, 3, 4, 5, 6\}$, which can be represented by the symbols $x_1, \ldots, x_6$. For a fair die, all 6 outcome values are equally probable, so the probability of each outcome value is $p(x_i) = 1/6$.

Using Equation 3.3, this probability distribution has entropy

$$H(X) \quad = \quad \sum_{i=1}^{6} p(x_i) \log \frac{1}{p(x_i)}, \tag{3.14}$$

where $\log 1/(1/6) = \log 6 = 2.585$, so that

$$H(X) \quad = \quad \sum_{i=1}^{6} \frac{1}{6} \times 2.585 \tag{3.15}$$

$$= \quad 2.585 \text{ bits.} \tag{3.16}$$

In words, each die outcome provides 2.585 bits of information. Because the entropy is the average information provided by each outcome, and because in this case each outcome provides the same amount of information, the entropy of a fair 6-sided die is also 2.585 bits.

> **Key Point.** The entropy of a variable X with m equiprobable outcome values is $H(X) = \log m$ bits.

The Entropy of a Pair of Dice

Throwing a pair of fair 6-sided dice yields an outcome in the form of an ordered pair of numbers, and there are a total of 36 equiprobable outcomes, as shown in Table 3.1. If we define an outcome value as the sum of one of these pairs of numbers then there are $N = 11$

possible outcome values, $A_x = \{2, 3, 4, 5, 6, 7, 8, 9, 10, 11, 12\}$, which can be represented by the symbols $x_1, \ldots, x_{11}$. Dividing the frequency of each outcome value x_i by 36 yields the probability $p(x_i)$ of that outcome value, as shown in Figure 3.3b and Table 3.1. Using these 11 probabilities in Equation 3.3, we can find the entropy:

$$
\begin{aligned}
H(X) &= \sum_{i=1}^{11} p(x_i) \log \frac{1}{p(x_i)} & (3.17) \\
&= p(x_1) \log \frac{1}{p(x_1)} + p(x_2) \log \frac{1}{p(x_2)} + \cdots + p(x_{11}) \log \frac{1}{p(x_{11})} \\
&= 3.27 \text{ bits.} & (3.18)
\end{aligned}
$$

3.3. Interpreting Entropy

We already know that the entropy of a coin being $H(X) = 1$ bit means that the variable X can be used to represent $m = 2^{H(X)} = 2^1 = 2$ equiprobable outcome values. By analogy, a variable with an entropy of $H(X)$ bits can be used to represent

$$
m = 2^{H(X)} \text{ equiprobable outcome values.} \qquad (3.19)
$$

For the 8-sided die considered above, the entropy of the distribution of outcome values is $H(X) = 3$ bits, which could therefore represent $2^3 = 8$ equiprobable values; this is consistent with the fact that the die has 8 sides. Similarly, a 6-sided die has entropy $H(X) = 2.585$

(a)

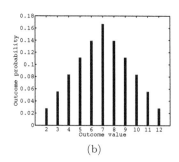

(b)

Figure 3.3: (a) A pair of dice. (b) Probability distribution of outcome values for a pair of dice.

bits, which could represent $2^{2.585} = 6$ equiprobable values, and this is consistent with the fact that the die has 6 sides.

In the case of the two dice, the entropy of the distribution of outcome values is $H(X) = 3.27$ bits, which could therefore represent $2^{3.27} = 9.65$ equiprobable values, as if we had a die with 9.65 sides. In other words, a pair of 6-sided dice has the same entropy as a single die with 9.65 sides. Similarly, the biased coin with $H(X) = 0.47$ bits (Equation 3.9) could be used to represent $m = 2^{0.47}$ or 1.38 equiprobable values, as if we had a die with 1.38 sides.

At first sight, these statements seem strange. Nevertheless, translating entropy into an equivalent number of equiprobable values can serve as an intuitive guide as to the amount of information provided by a variable.

Key Point. Entropy is average information. A variable with an entropy of $H(X)$ bits provides enough information to choose between $m = 2^{H(X)}$ equiprobable values.

Symbol	Sum	Outcome	Frequency	$p(x_i)$	Surprisal
x_1	2	1:1	1	0.03	5.17
x_2	3	1:2, 2:1	2	0.06	4.17
x_3	4	1:3, 3:1, 2:2	3	0.08	3.59
x_4	5	2:3, 3:2, 1:4, 4:1	4	0.11	3.17
x_5	6	2:4, 4:2, 1:5, 5:1, 3:3	5	0.14	2.85
x_6	7	3:4, 4:3, 2:5, 5:2, 1:6, 6:1	6	0.17	2.59
x_7	8	3:5, 5:3, 2:6, 6:2, 4:4	5	0.14	2.85
x_8	9	3:6, 6:3, 4:5, 5:4	4	0.11	3.17
x_9	10	4:6, 6:4, 5:5	3	0.08	3.59
x_{10}	11	5:6, 6:5	2	0.06	4.17
x_{11}	12	6:6	1	0.03	5.17

Table 3.1: A pair of dice has 36 possible outcomes, each represented by an ordered pair of numbers separated with a colon. The outcome value is the sum of the two numbers in a pair, i.e. the total number of dots for a given throw of the dice. Each of the 11 distinct outcome values is represented by a symbol x_i. The frequency of each x_i is the number of different outcomes that yield the sum x_i, and $p(x_i)$, the probability that the pair of dice yields a given outcome value x_i, is given by the frequency divided by 36. The surprisal of outcome value x_i is $p(x_i) \log 1/p(x_i)$ bits.

Entropy: Give and Take

Entropy is a measure of *uncertainty*. When our uncertainty is reduced, we gain information, and vice versa, so information and entropy are two sides of the same coin. However, information has a rather subtle interpretation, which can easily lead to confusion.

Average information and entropy share the same definition, but whether we call a given quantity information or entropy usually depends on whether it is being given to us or taken away. For example, if a variable has high entropy then our initial uncertainty about its value is large and is, by definition, exactly equal to its entropy. If we are told the value of that variable then, on average, we have been given an amount of information equal to the uncertainty (entropy) we initially had about its value. Thus, receiving an amount of information is equivalent to having exactly the same amount of entropy taken away.

> **Key point**. If a variable has an entropy of $H(X)$ bits then our initial uncertainty about its value is $H(X)$ bits. If we are told the value of X then, on average, we have been given $H(X)$ bits of information.

Chapter 4

Entropy of Continuous Variables

4.1. The Trouble with Entropy

So far, we have considered entropy in the context of discrete random variables (e.g. coin flipping). However, we also need a definition of entropy for continuous random variables (e.g. length). It is often the case that results obtained with discrete variables can easily be extended to continuous variables, but information theory is not one of those cases. Fortunately, there are ways to generalise the discrete definition of entropy to obtain sensible measures of entropy for continuous variables [16;23;26;28;38].

To estimate the entropy of any variable, it is necessary to know the probability associated with each of its possible values. For a continuous variable this amounts to knowing its *probability density function*, or *pdf*, which we refer to here as its distribution. We can use a pdf as a starting point for estimating the entropy of a continuous variable by making a histogram of a large number of measured values. However, this reveals a fundamental problem, as we shall see below.

In order to make a histogram of values for any continuous quantity X, such as human height, we need to define the width Δx of bins in the histogram. We then categorise each measured value of X into one histogram bin, as in Figure 4.1. Then the probability that a randomly chosen value x of X is in a given bin is simply the proportion of values of X in that bin. The entropy of this histogram is then given by the average surprisal of its bins,

$$H(X^\Delta) = \sum_i (\text{prob } x \text{ is in } i\text{th bin}) \times \log \frac{1}{(\text{prob } x \text{ is in } i\text{th bin})}, \quad (4.1)$$

where $X^\triangle$ indicates that we are dealing with a continuous variable X which has been discretised using a histogram in which each bin has width Δx, as in Figure 4.1. We have purposely not specified the number of bins, which can be infinite in principle.

The probability that a randomly chosen value of X is in the ith bin is given by the area a_i of the ith column expressed as a proportion of the total area A of all columns. A bin that contains n_i values has a column area equal to its height n_i times its width Δx, $a_i = n_i \times \Delta x$. Given that the sum of all column areas is $A = \sum_i a_i$, the probability that X is in the ith bin is the proportion of area occupied by the ith column, $P_i = a_i/A$. It will prove useful later to note that the sum of these proportions (i.e. total area) is necessarily equal to 1:

$$\sum_i P_i \;=\; 1. \tag{4.2}$$

We can now rewrite Equation 4.1 more succinctly as

$$H(X^\triangle) \;=\; \sum_i P_i \log \frac{1}{P_i}. \tag{4.3}$$

If we divide values on the vertical axis of the histogram by A then the ith column in the resultant *normalised histogram* has height n_i/A and area $n_i/A \times \Delta x = a_i/A = P_i$, so the total area of the normalised

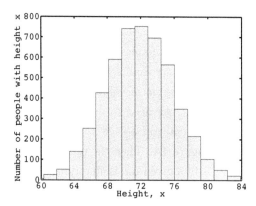

Figure 4.1: A histogram of $n = 5{,}000$ hypothetical values of human height X, measured in inches. This histogram was constructed by dividing values of X into a number of intervals or bins, where each bin has width Δx, and then counting how many measured values are in each bin.

histogram is $\sum_i P_i = 1$. If we write the height of the ith column in this normalised histogram as $p(x_i)$ then its area is

$$P_i = p(x_i)\,\Delta x, \tag{4.4}$$

which is the probability that the value of X is in the ith bin, so $p(x_i) = P_i/\Delta x$ can be interpreted as a *probability density*.

Substituting Equation 4.4 into Equation 4.3 yields

$$H(X^\Delta) = \sum_i p(x_i)\Delta x \times \log \frac{1}{p(x_i)\Delta x}. \tag{4.5}$$

By the laws of logarithms, the final term can be written as

$$\log \frac{1}{p(x_i)\,\Delta x} = \log \frac{1}{p(x_i)} + \log \frac{1}{\Delta x}, \tag{4.6}$$

so we can rewrite Equation 4.5 as

$$H(X^\Delta) = \left[\sum_i p(x_i)\,\Delta x \log \frac{1}{p(x_i)}\right] + \left[\log \frac{1}{\Delta x}\sum_i P_i\right].$$

According to Equation 4.2, $\sum P_i = 1$; therefore

$$H(X^\Delta) = \left[\sum_i p(x_i)\,\Delta x \log \frac{1}{p(x_i)}\right] + \log \frac{1}{\Delta x}. \tag{4.7}$$

As the bin width Δx approaches zero, the first term on the right becomes an integral, but the second term diverges to infinity, giving

$$H(X) = \left[\int_{x=-\infty}^{\infty} p(x) \log \frac{1}{p(x)}\,dx\right] + \infty. \tag{4.8}$$

And there's the problem: for a continuous variable, as the bin width Δx approaches zero, $1/\Delta x$, and hence $\log(1/\Delta x)$, and therefore the entropy of X, diverges to infinity.

Key point. The entropy $H(X^\Delta)$ of a (discretised) continuous variable increases as the width of bins in that variable's histogram decreases.

4.2. Differential Entropy

Equation 4.8 states that the entropy of a continuous variable is infinite, which is true but not very helpful. If all continuous variables have infinite entropy then distributions that are obviously different would have the same (infinite) entropy (see Chapter 5 for three different pdfs).

A measure of entropy called the *differential entropy* of a continuous variable ignores this infinity; it is defined as

$$H_{\text{dif}}(X) \quad = \quad \int_{x=-\infty}^{\infty} p(x) \log \frac{1}{p(x)} \, dx, \qquad (4.9)$$

where the subscript 'dif' stands for 'differential' (although it is omitted when the intended meaning is unambiguous). Thus, the differential entropy is that part of the entropy which includes only the 'interesting' part of Equation 4.8.

Key point. The entropy of a continuous variable is infinite because it includes a constant term that is infinite. If we ignore this term then we obtain the *differential entropy* $H_{\text{dif}}(X) = E[\log(1/p(x))]$, the mean value of $\log(1/p(x))$.

4.3. What is Half a Bit of Information?

If a variable has a uniform distribution (i.e. all values are equiprobable, as with a fair coin or die) then receiving one bit halves our uncertainty about its value, just as it halves the number of possible routes in Figure 2.1. However, we often encounter fractions of a bit. What does it mean to have, say, half a bit of information?

We can find out what a fraction of a bit means by copying the recipe we use for whole bits (Equation 3.19). For clarity, we assume that the variable X has a uniform distribution and that we know nothing about the value of X. For example, the distribution of the fair 8-sided die shown in Figure 3.2b has an entropy of three bits; its outcome can be any one of 8 values, and this corresponds to an initial uncertainty of 100%. If we are given $H = 2$ bits of information about the value

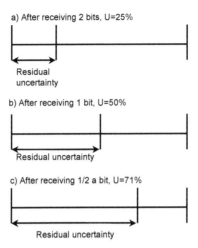

Figure 4.2: If we have no information about the location of a point on a line of length 1 then our uncertainty is $U = 100\%$. (a) After receiving 2 bits, $U = 2^{-2} = 25\%$, so we know which interval of length 0.25 contains the point. (b) After receiving 1 bit, $U = 2^{-1} = 50\%$, so we know which region of length 0.5 contains the point. (c) After receiving 1/2 bit, $U = 2^{-1/2} = 71\%$, so we know which region of length 0.71 contains the point.

of X, this reduces our uncertainty by a factor of $2^H = 2^2 = 4$, so our uncertainty about the value of X is one quarter as much as it was before receiving these 2 bits. Because the die has 8 sides, we now know that the outcome can be one of only two possible values (e.g. 3 or 7). More generally, if we treat our initial uncertainty as 100%, after receiving 2 bits our *residual uncertainty* is $U = 25\%$, as shown in Figure 4.2. Note that the term residual uncertainty is unique to this book.

Now consider how this reasoning might apply to a continuous quantity, such as the position of a point on a line of length 1. Initially, our uncertainty spans the whole line. After receiving 2 bits, the region representing the residual uncertainty has a length of 0.25 (see Figure 4.2). The precise location of this region depends on the particular information received, just as the particular set of possible values for the outcome of the 8-sided die depends on the information received.

The recipe we have just used (Equation 3.19) applies to any amount of information H, for which the residual uncertainty after receiving this information is

$$U = 2^{-H}, \tag{4.10}$$

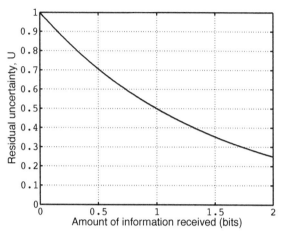

Figure 4.3: Residual uncertainty U after receiving different amounts of information H, where $U = 2^{-H}$.

as shown in Figure 4.3. So, if we have $H = 1$ bit then our residual uncertainty is $U = 2^{-1} = 1/2 = 50\%$, half as much as it was before receiving this 1 bit. Analogously, if we receive half a bit of information then our residual uncertainty is $U = 2^{-1/2} = 0.71 = 71\%$ as much as it was before we received that information.

Let's keep this half a bit, and let's call our residual uncertainty $U_1 = 0.71$. If we are given another half a bit then our uncertainty will again be reduced by a factor of 0.71. Thus, after being given two half bits, our new residual uncertainty is $U_2 = 0.71 \times U_1 = 0.5$. So, as we should expect, being given two half bits yields the same residual uncertainty (0.5) as being given one bit. Notice that this provides a good example of how Shannon's definition of information meets the additivity condition stated in the desiderata of Section 2.4.

> **Key point.** A complete uncertainty of $U = 100\%$ is reduced to a residual uncertainty of $U = 2^{-0.5} = 71\%$ after receiving half a bit of information. In general, the residual uncertainty is $U = 2^{-H}$ after receiving H bits.

Chapter 5

Maximum Entropy Distributions

5.1. Why Maximum Entropy?

A distribution of values that has as much entropy as theoretically possible is a *maximum entropy distribution*. The reason we are interested in maximum entropy distributions is because entropy equates to information, so a maximum entropy distribution is also a *maximum information distribution*. In other words, the amount of information conveyed by each value from a maximum entropy distribution is as large as it can possibly be. This matters because if we have some quantity S with a particular distribution $p(S)$ and we wish to transmit S through a communication channel, then we had better transform (encode) S into another variable X with a maximum entropy distribution $p(X)$ before it is transmitted.

For a given variable, the precise form of its maximum entropy distribution depends on the constraints placed on the values of that variable[28]. Three important examples of maximum entropy distributions are described below.

5.2. The Uniform Distribution

Consider a random variable X that is distributed uniformly between 0 and a, so the probability density $p(x)$ has the same value for all values x of X, as in Figure 5.1 for $a = 2$. By definition, the area of the distribution $p(X)$ must equal 1, i.e. $p(x) \times a = 1$, so the probability density function of a uniform distribution is

$$
p(x) \quad = \quad
\begin{cases}
\frac{1}{a} & \text{for } 0 < x < a, \\
0 & \text{otherwise.}
\end{cases}
\tag{5.1}
$$

A random variable X with a uniform distribution that is non-zero between 0 and a is written as $X \sim U(0, a)$. The entropy of this distribution is therefore

$$
\begin{aligned}
H_{\text{dif}}(X) &= \int_{x=-\infty}^{\infty} p(x) \log \frac{1}{p(x)} \, dx \\[2mm]
&= \int_{x=0}^{a} \frac{1}{a} \log a \, dx & (5.2) \\[2mm]
&= a \times \frac{1}{a} \log a = \log a \text{ bits.} & (5.3)
\end{aligned}
$$

Strictly speaking, this is the differential entropy, but we call it simply the entropy for brevity. This result is intuitively consistent with the entropy of discrete variables. In the case of a discrete variable, we know from Equation 2.2 that doubling the number of possible outcome values increases the entropy of the variable by one (i.e. $\log 2$) bit. Similarly, for a continuous variable with a uniform distribution, doubling the range of the distribution effectively doubles the number of possible outcome values (provided we are content to accept that this number is infinitely large for a continuous variable) and also increases the entropy of that variable by one bit. For example, if the upper limit of X values is increased from a to $b = 2a$ then the entropy of the variable $Y = 2X$ is

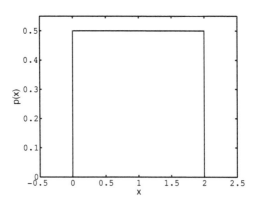

Figure 5.1: A uniform distribution with a range between 0 and 2 has an area of 1 ($= 2 \times 0.5$) and an entropy of $\log 2 = 1$ bit.

exactly one bit greater than the entropy of X:

$$H_{\text{dif}}(Y) = \log b = \log 2a = \log 2 + \log a = \log a + 1 \text{ bits.} \quad (5.4)$$

More importantly, for continuous variables that have fixed lower and upper bounds (e.g. 0 and a), *no probability distribution can have a greater entropy than the uniform distribution*[28].

> **Key point.** Given a variable X with fixed lower and upper bounds, the maximum entropy distribution is the uniform distribution.

An odd feature of the entropy of a continuous distribution is that it can be zero or *negative*. In the case of $X \sim U(0, a)$, if $a = 1$ then $H_{\text{dif}}(X) = 0$, and if $a = 0.5$ then $H_{\text{dif}}(X) = -1$. One way to think about this is to interpret the entropy of any uniform distribution relative to the entropy of a uniform distribution with entropy $H_{\text{dif}}(X) = 0$ (i.e. with a range of $a = 1$).

For example, a uniform distribution with $a = 2$ has an entropy that is $H_{\text{dif}}(X) = 1$ bit larger than the entropy of a distribution with $a = 1$. And a uniform distribution with $a = 0.5$ has an entropy that is one bit smaller than that of a distribution with $a = 1$.

5.3. The Exponential Distribution

An exponential distribution is defined by one parameter: its *mean*, μ. The probability density function of a variable with an exponential distribution is

$$p(x) = \begin{cases} \frac{1}{\mu} e^{-\frac{x}{\mu}} & \text{for } x \geq 0, \\ 0 & \text{for } x < 0, \end{cases} \quad (5.5)$$

as shown in Figure 5.2 for $\mu = 1$, where the constant e is Euler's number ($e \approx 2.718$). By convention, a random variable X with an exponential distribution that has a mean of μ is written as $X \sim \exp(\mu)$. The

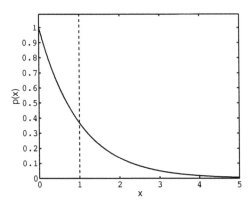

Figure 5.2: An exponential distribution with a mean of $\mu = 1$ (indicated by the vertical dashed line) has an entropy of $H_{\mathrm{dif}}(X) = 1.44$ bits. entropy of an exponential distribution is[28]

$$H_{\mathrm{dif}}(X) \quad = \quad \log\left(e\mu\right) \text{ bits.} \tag{5.6}$$

More importantly, if we know nothing about a variable X except that it is positive and that its mean value is μ then the distribution of X with the maximum entropy is the exponential distribution.

> **Key point.** Given a positive variable X that has a fixed mean μ but is otherwise unconstrained, the maximum entropy distribution is the exponential distribution.

5.4. The Gaussian Distribution

A Gaussian distribution is defined by two parameters, its *mean* μ and its *variance* v, which is the square of its *standard deviation* σ, so $v = \sigma^2$ (see Figure 5.3). The probability density function of a variable with a Gaussian distribution is

$$p(x) \quad = \quad \frac{1}{\sigma\sqrt{2\pi}} e^{-\frac{(x-\mu)^2}{2\sigma^2}}, \tag{5.7}$$

where the mean determines the location of the peak of the probability distribution and the standard deviation determines how spread out the distribution is. By convention, a random variable X with a Gaussian

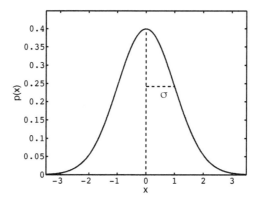

Figure 5.3: A Gaussian distribution with a mean of $\mu = 0$ and a standard deviation of $\sigma = 1$ (indicated by the horizontal dashed line) has an entropy of $H_{\text{dif}} = 2.05$ bits.

distribution that has mean μ and variance v is written as $X \sim \mathcal{N}(\mu, v)$. The entropy of a Gaussian variable is[28]

$$
\begin{aligned}
H_{\text{dif}}(X) \quad &= \quad \tfrac{1}{2} \log \left(2\pi e \sigma^2 \right) && (5.8) \\
&= \quad \tfrac{1}{2} \log \left(2\pi e \right) + \log \sigma && (5.9) \\
&\approx \quad 2.05 + \log \sigma \quad \text{bits.} && (5.10)
\end{aligned}
$$

Since $\log 1 = 0$, a Gaussian distribution with a standard deviation of $\sigma = 1$ has an entropy of 2.05 bits. Notice that the entropy of X depends on how spread out the distribution $p(X)$ is (as determined by σ), but is independent of its location (as determined by μ). If a variable X is constrained to have a fixed variance σ^2 then *no probability distribution can have a greater entropy than the Gaussian distribution*[28].

Key point. Given a variable X that has a fixed standard deviation σ but is otherwise unconstrained, the maximum entropy distribution is the Gaussian distribution.

Chapter 6

Noiseless Channels

Our objective is to transmit a message reliably through a communication channel as shown in Figure 6.1. The message or *source signal s* is a physical quantity, such as a sound or an image. This source signal is encoded as the channel input x. After the encoded message has been transmitted through the channel, the output y is decoded in an attempt to recover the message s. The channel capacity C is the maximum amount of information that the channel can provide at its output about the input.

Key point. The *channel capacity C* is the maximum amount of information that a channel's output can provide about its input value, usually expressed in bits per second.

6.1. The Source Coding Theorem

Shannon's source coding theorem, described below, applies only to noiseless channels. This theorem is really about repackaging (encoding) data before they are transmitted so that, when transmitted, every encoded datum conveys as much information as possible. We will discuss the source coding theorem using binary digits, but the argument applies equally well to any type of channel input.

Given that each binary digit can convey a maximum of one bit of information (see Figure 3.1), a noiseless channel that communicates R binary digits per second can communicate information at a rate of up to R bits/s. Because the channel capacity C is the maximum rate at which information can be transmitted from input to output, the capacity of a noiseless channel is numerically equal to the number R of binary digits communicated per second. However, if each binary digit carries less than one bit (which would be the case if consecutive output values are correlated; see Section 6.3) then the rate R is less than the channel capacity C.

Suppose that a source generates a stream of data in the form of signal values $s_1, s_2, \ldots$, with an entropy of $H(S)$ bits per value, and a channel transmits the corresponding encoded inputs $x_1, x_2, \ldots$, where each input consists of C binary digits. *Shannon's source coding theorem* guarantees that if any source signal has entropy $H(S)$ then, upon averaging over all source signals,

a) an average of (at most, just over) $H(S)$ binary digits are required to encode each value of s, and

b) on average, each value of s cannot be encoded using any fewer than $H(S)$ binary digits.

Recalling the example of the two dice from Section 3.2, if all 11 outcome values were equiprobable then a naive encoding would require an average of $\log 11 = 3.46$ binary digits to represent each outcome value. However, we know that the entropy of the distribution of outcome values is only $H(X) = 3.27$ bits. Shannon's source coding theorem guarantees that for a variable with an entropy of $H(X) = 3.27$ bits, an encoding exists such that an average of (just over) 3.27 binary digits per outcome value will suffice (the phrase 'just over' is short-hand for the more precise phrase 'arbitrarily close to', used below).

The encoding process yields inputs with a specific distribution $p(X)$, where there are implicit constraints on the form of $p(X)$ (e.g. power constraints). The shape of the distribution $p(X)$ places an upper limit

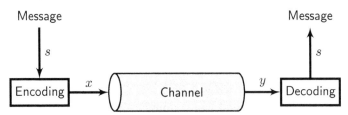

Figure 6.1: The noiseless communication channel. A message (data) is encoded before being used as input to a communication channel. The channel output is decoded by a receiver to recover the message.

on the entropy $H(X)$ and therefore on the maximum information that an average input can carry. Thus, the capacity of a noiseless channel is defined in terms of the particular distribution $p(X)$ that maximises the average amount of information per input:

$$C = \max_{p(X)} H(X) \text{ bits/s.} \qquad (6.1)$$

This states that the channel capacity C is given by the distribution $p(X)$ which makes $H(X)$ as large as possible (see Section 5.1).

Shannon's Source Coding Theorem

Now that we are familiar with the core concepts of information theory, we can quote Shannon's source coding theorem in full. This is also known as Shannon's *fundamental theorem for a discrete noiseless channel* and as the *first fundamental coding theorem*.

> Let a source have entropy H (bits per symbol) and a channel have a capacity C (bits per second). Then it is possible to encode the output of the source in such a way as to transmit at the average rate $C/H - \epsilon$ symbols per second over the channel where ϵ is arbitrarily small. It is not possible to transmit at an average rate greater than C/H [symbols/s]. Shannon and Weaver, 1949[35].

This somewhat terse theorem can be made more accessible, as follows. If ϵ is arbitrarily small then the transmission rate is arbitrarily close to C/H symbols/s. And, given that each symbol conveys H bits, the rate expressed in bits/s can be arbitrarily close to

$$(H \text{ bits/symbol}) \times (C/H \text{ symbols/s}) = C \text{ bits/s,} \qquad (6.2)$$

which is the channel capacity. In other words, Shannon's source coding theorem implies that it is possible to encode the output of a source in such a way as to transmit at an average rate arbitrarily close to the channel capacity of C bits/s. This, in turn, implies that the maximum number of binary digits required to encode messages with an entropy of H bits is arbitrarily close to (i.e. just over) H binary digits.

6.2. Why the Theorem is True

Consider an encoded message $\mathbf{x} = (x_1, \ldots, x_n)$. The number of encoded messages of length n that contain n_1 1s and n_0 0s is just the number of different ways of distributing n_1 1s and n_0 0s over n positions. This can be calculated as a *binomial coefficient*,

$$C_{n,n_1} \quad = \quad \frac{n!}{n_1!\,n_0!}, \tag{6.3}$$

where $n! = n \times (n-1) \times \cdots \times 1$. When considered over all values between $n_1 = 0$ and $n_1 = n$, the total number of possible distinct encoded messages is

$$\sum_{n_1=0}^{n} C_{n,n_1} \quad = \quad 2^n, \tag{6.4}$$

which is reassuring, given that there are 2^n possible encoded messages.

If the probability that each binary digit equals 1 is p_1 then the probability that each binary digit equals 0 is $p_0 = 1 - p_1$. As n increases, the law of large numbers ensures that almost all encoded messages contain $n_1 = np_1$ 1s and $n_0 = np_0$ 0s. Thus, for all practical purposes, the number of distinct encoded messages is (just over)

$$m \quad = \quad C_{n,n_1}. \tag{6.5}$$

Our plan is to find the logarithm of C_{n,n_1}, and, in so doing, we will confirm that it is the entropy of the encoded messages. This is achieved by using *Stirling's approximation*, which states that if n is large then

$$\ln n! \quad \approx \quad n[(\ln n) - 1], \tag{6.6}$$

where $\ln$ denotes the natural logarithm (i.e. the logarithm to base $e \approx 2.718$). We begin with the natural logarithm of Equation 6.5:

$$\ln m \quad = \quad \ln C_{n,n_1} \tag{6.7}$$

$$= \quad \ln n! - \ln n_1! - \ln n_0!. \tag{6.8}$$

Then Stirling's approximation yields

$$\ln m \quad \approx \quad n[(\ln n) - 1] - n_1[(\ln n_1) - 1] - n_0[(\ln n_0) - 1] \quad (6.9)$$

$$= \quad n \ln n - n_1 \ln n_1 - n_0 \ln n_0 - (n - (n_1 + n_0)). \quad (6.10)$$

Given that $n = n_0 + n_1$, this can be rewritten as

$$\ln m \quad \approx \quad (n_0 + n_1) \ln n - n_1 \ln n_1 - n_0 \ln n_0 \quad (6.11)$$

$$= \quad n_1(\ln n - \ln n_1) + n_0(\ln n - \ln n_0) \quad (6.12)$$

$$= \quad n \left(\left[\frac{n_1}{n} \ln \frac{n}{n_1} \right] + \left[\frac{n_0}{n} \ln \frac{n}{n_0} \right] \right). \quad (6.13)$$

Because we are assuming that n is large (as required by Stirling's approximation), it is almost certain that each message contains exactly np_1 1s and np_0 0s; therefore $n_1/n \approx p_1$ and $n_0/n \approx p_0$, so that

$$\ln m \quad \approx \quad n \left(p_1 \ln \frac{1}{p_1} + p_0 \ln \frac{1}{p_0} \right). \quad (6.14)$$

We can recognise the sum in brackets as the entropy $H(X)$ of a variable X with two possible values (see Equation 3.10), so n times this is the entropy of the encoded message $\mathbf{x} = (x_1, \ldots, x_n)$. However, because we have used natural logarithms, this entropy is expressed in units called *nats*. If we use logarithms to base 2 then we obtain the entropy in units of bits, and we find that the encoded message $\mathbf{x}$ has an average of

$$\log_2 m \quad \approx \quad n \left(p_1 \log_2 \frac{1}{p_1} + p_0 \log_2 \frac{1}{p_0} \right) \quad (6.15)$$

$$= \quad n \sum_{i=0}^{1} p_i \log_2 \frac{1}{p_i} \quad (6.16)$$

$$= \quad n H(X) \text{ bits per message.} \quad (6.17)$$

The preceding account is not a rigorous proof of Shannon's source coding theorem, but it conveys the key ideas that underpin the proofs presented by Shannon and others (e.g. MacKay, 2003[20]).

6.3. A Picture of Information

Suppose we want to transmit an image of 100×100 pixels, in which each pixel can adopt one out of 256 possible grey-level values, as in Figure 6.2a. If we were to send each pixel's value individually, we would need to send 10,000 values. Because each value could be anywhere between 0 and 255, we could represent each pixel's value as a binary number containing eight binary digits ($8 = \log 256$).

However, there are large regions of the image that look as if they contain only one grey-level value. In fact, each such region contains values that are similar but not identical, as shown in Figure 6.3. The similarity between adjacent pixel values means that the value of one pixel can be predicted (to some extent) by the values of nearby pixels. This, in turn, means that adjacent pixel values are not *independent* of each other (specifically, not iid), so the image has a degree of *redundancy*. How can this observation be used to encode the image using fewer than eight binary digits per pixel?

One method consists of encoding the image in terms of the differences between the grey-levels of adjacent pixels. For brevity, we will call this *difference coding*. In principle, the differences could be measured in any direction within the image, but for simplicity we first concatenate consecutive rows to form a single row of 10,000 pixels, and then take

(a)   (b)

Figure 6.2: Grey-level image. (a) An image in which each pixel adopts one out of 256 possible grey-levels, between 0 and 255, each of which can be represented by a binary number with 8 binary digits (e.g. 255 = 11111111). (b) Histogram of grey-levels in the picture.

the difference between each pair of adjacent grey-levels. The result of this difference coding can be seen in Figure 6.4a.

If two adjacent pixel values are similar then their difference is close to zero. In fact, the histogram of difference values shown in Figure 6.4b shows that the most common difference values are indeed close to zero, and difference values are only rarely greater than ±63. Thus, using difference coding, we could represent almost every one of the 9999 difference values in Figure 6.4a as a number between −63 and +63. Incidentally, coding procedures have special 'housekeeping' fragments of computer code to deal with values outside the range ±63, which incur negligible extra cost.

At first glance, it may not be obvious how difference coding represents any saving over simply sending each pixel's grey-level value. However, because these differences are between −63 and +63, they span a range of 127 different values, $\{-63, -62, \ldots, 0, \ldots, 62, 63\}$. Any number in this range can be represented using seven binary digits, because $7 = \log 128$ (which leaves one spare value).

Once we have encoded an image into a sequence of 9999 pixel difference values $(d_1, d_2, \ldots, d_{9999})$, how do we use them to reconstruct the original image? Well, if the difference d_1 between the first pixel value x_1 and the second pixel value x_2 is, say, $d_1 = x_2 - x_1 = 10$ and the value of x_1 is 5, then we obtain the value of x_2 by adding 10 to x_1; that is, $x_2 = x_1 + d_1 = 5 + 10 = 15$. We then do the same for the third pixel $(x_3 = x_2 + d_2)$ and continue this process for all subsequent pixels.

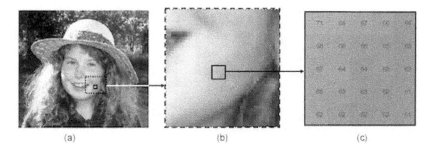

(a)   (b)   (c)

Figure 6.3: Adjacent pixels tend to have similar grey-levels, so the image has a large amount of redundancy, which can be used for efficient encoding. (a) Grey-level image.   (b) Magnified square from a.   (c) Magnified square from b, with individual pixel grey-levels indicated.

Thus, provided we know the value of the first pixel in the original image (which can be encoded using eight binary digits), we can use these pixel value differences to recover the value of every pixel in the original image. The fact that we can reconstruct the original image (Figure 6.2a) from the set of pixel value differences (Figure 6.4a) proves that they contain exactly the same amount of information.

Let's work out the total saving from using this difference coding method. The naive method of sending all 10,000 pixel values, which can take values between 0 and 255, would need eight binary digits per pixel, requiring a total of 80,000 binary digits. But by using difference coding we would need seven binary digits for each of the 9,999 difference values, plus eight binary digits for the first pixel value, making a total of only 70,001 binary digits.

A histogram of data values (e.g. pixel grey-levels) can be used to obtain an upper bound on the average amount of information (entropy) each data value could convey (the entropy would equal this upper bound if pixel values were iid). It turns out that the histogram (Figure 6.2b) of the grey-levels in Figure 6.2a yields an upper bound of 7.84 bits/pixel, while the histogram (Figure 6.4b) of the grey-level differences in Figure 6.4a yields an upper bound of just 5.92 bits/pixel.

Given that the images in Figures 6.2a and 6.4a contain the same amount of information, and that Figure 6.4a contains no more than 5.92 bits/pixel, it follows that Figure 6.2a cannot contain more than

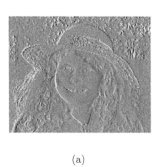

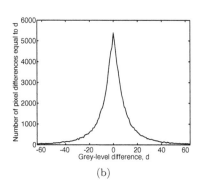

(a)   (b)

Figure 6.4: Difference coding. (a) Each pixel value is the difference between adjacent horizontal grey-level values in Figure 6.2a (grey = zero difference). (b) Histogram of grey-level differences between adjacent pixel grey-levels in Figure 6.2a; only differences between ±63 are plotted.

5.92 bits/pixel either. This matters because Shannon's source coding theorem guarantees that if each pixel's grey-level contains an average of 5.92 bits of information then (in principle) we should be able to represent Figure 6.2a using just over 5.92 binary digits per pixel.

Key point. Shannon's source coding theorem guarantees that if each pixel in Figure 6.2a represents an average of $H(X) = 5.92$ bits of information then it is possible to store that image using an average of (just over) 5.92 binary digits per pixel.

But the estimate of 5.92 bits/pixel is still an upper bound. In fact, the smallest number of binary digits needed to represent each pixel is numerically equal to the average amount of information (in bits) implicit in each pixel. So if we want to know the smallest number of binary digits that could be used to represent each pixel grey-level then what we really need to find out is how many bits of information each pixel represents.

This is a hard question, but we can get an idea of the answer by comparing the amount of computer memory required to represent the image in two different contexts.

First, to display the image on a computer screen, the value of each pixel requires eight binary digits of computer memory, so the bigger the picture, the more memory it requires to be displayed.

Second, a compressed version of the image can be stored on the computer's hard drive using fewer than eight binary digits per pixel. We have already seen that by a simple method (difference coding) we can represent each pixel with only seven binary digits, but more conventional methods used in compression algorithms (e.g. *gzip*) can represent each pixel with even fewer binary digits. Consequently, storing the compressed version of an image on the computer's hard drive requires less memory than displaying that image on the screen.

For example, if the image in Figure 6.2a has 10,000 pixels, where each pixel's grey-level value is between 0 and 255, then each pixel can be represented on a computer screen using eight binary digits (because $2^8 = 256$) or one *byte*, so the entire image can be represented using

10,000 bytes. However, when the gzipped file containing this image is inspected, it is typically found to contain only 5,000 bytes; in other words, the image in Figure 6.2a has been compressed by a factor of 2 (= 10,000/5,000). This means that the information implicit in each pixel, which requires eight binary digits for it to be displayed on a screen, can be represented with only four binary digits on a computer's hard drive.

This is important because it implies that each set of eight binary digits used to display each pixel of Figure 6.2a represents an average of only four bits of information; therefore each binary digit that contributes to displaying one pixel corresponds to an average of only *half a bit* of information. At first sight, this seems like an odd statement. But, as discussed in Section 4.3, a fraction of a bit is a well-defined quantity, with a reasonably intuitive interpretation.

Chapter 7

Mutual Information and Noise

7.1. Noise

Let's begin with a really simple example. Imagine you use your computer to send an email that says, "Meet me at 8, and don't be late." You type the letters *M*, *e*, *e* and *t*, and then you glance at the screen to see the word *Neet*. Either you hit the wrong key, or the computer made an error, so there are at least two possible explanations.

The first explanation is that your brain intended to type *M*, but the message from your brain to your finger had to travel through several feet of nerve fibres before reaching your finger, and the message got corrupted along the way by a small amount of random noise. This noise altered the message just enough for your finger to hit the wrong key.

The second explanation is you hit the correct key, but the message from the keyboard to the computer had to travel through a length of cable before reaching the computer, and the message got corrupted along the way by a small amount of random noise. This noise altered the message just enough for the computer to display the letter *N* instead of *M*.

Whichever explanation is correct, in both cases the problem is that the message got corrupted by noise as it travelled from the sender (your brain or the keyboard) to the receiver (your finger or the computer). Indeed, the problem of noise lies at the heart of information theory. An obvious solution is to simply eliminate noise. Unfortunately, noise is everywhere. There is no measurement you can make, no signal you can receive, that does not contain some unwanted components in the form of noise. When you detune a radio, the hiss you hear is so-called white noise; and when you tune into a radio station, the noise does not disappear – it just becomes less audible.

Of course, noise is not restricted to radios, nerve fibres and computer keyboards. It occurs in wifi systems, satellite communications, TV signals, speech, and sensory perceptions of the world through eyes, ears and fingers.

So, what has this got to do with information theory? In essence, information theory tells us exactly how much information we can communicate as the amount of noise varies.

The *mutual information* between two variables, such as the input and output of a channel, is the average amount of information that each value of the output provides about the input. Somewhat counter-intuitively, this is the same as the average amount of information that each value of the input provides about the output.

Mutual information can be understood as follows. Before we receive an output y, our uncertainty about the input x (when averaged over all possible input values) can be summarised as the input entropy $H(X)$ (see Sections 3.3 and 4.3). After we receive an output y, our uncertainty should be reduced to some lower amount. This amount is the conditional entropy, $H(X|y)$, read as 'the uncertainty (entropy) in X given an output value y'. So, after receiving y, our uncertainty about the value of the input x is reduced from $H(X)$ to $H(X|y)$.

As discussed in Section 3.3, a reduction in uncertainty is equivalent to a gain in information. The exact amount of information gained is the

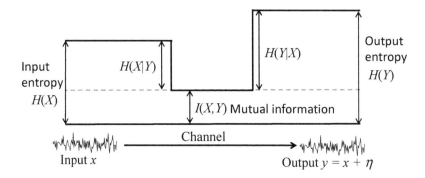

Figure 7.1: Relationships between information-theoretic quantities. The noise η in the output has entropy $H(\eta) = H(Y|X)$, which represents uncertainty in the output given the input. The noise in the input has entropy $H(X|Y)$, which represents uncertainty in the input given the output. The mutual information is $I(X,Y) = H(X) - H(X|Y) = H(Y) - H(Y|X)$ bits.

difference between the (usually large) uncertainty $H(X)$ we had before we received an output and the (usually smaller) uncertainty $H(X|y)$ we have after receiving an output. When averaged over all output values y, this difference is the mutual information between input and output,

$$I(X, Y) \quad = \quad H(X) - H(X|Y) \text{ bits.} \tag{7.1}$$

Thus, mutual information is the average uncertainty we had before receiving an output minus the average uncertainty we have after receiving an output. Consequently, receiving an output amounts to gaining an average of $I(X, Y)$ bits about the input.

If we swap the roles of the input X and the output Y then we obtain

$$I(Y, X) \quad = \quad H(Y) - H(Y|X) \text{ bits,} \tag{7.2}$$

which demonstrates the symmetric nature of mutual information. These relationships are illustrated in Figures 7.1, 7.2 and 7.3.

Key point. The mutual information between two variables X and Y is the average amount of information that each value of Y provides about X. It is also the average amount of information that each value of X provides about Y.

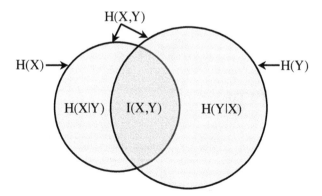

Figure 7.2: Mutual information between related variables X and Y. Each circle represents the entropy of one variable.

7.2. Joint Entropy

The probability that $X = x_i$ and that $Y = y_j$ is called the *joint probability* $p(x_i, y_j)$. When considered over all values of X and Y, these probabilities define a *joint probability distribution* $p(X, Y)$. The entropy of a joint probability distribution, the *joint entropy*, is a straightforward generalisation of the entropy of the distribution a single variable:

$$H(X,Y) = \sum_{i=1}^{m_x} \sum_{j=1}^{m_y} p(x_i, y_j) \log \frac{1}{p(x_i, y_j)} \tag{7.3}$$

$$= E\left[\log \frac{1}{p(x, y)}\right] \text{ bits per pair,} \tag{7.4}$$

where m_x is the number of different values of X and m_y is the number of different values of Y. The term *bits per pair* is used to emphasise the fact that the joint entropy $H(X, Y)$ is the average amount of Shannon information conveyed by each pair of values.

Note that each of the various entropy terms in this chapter represents a subset of the joint entropy, as shown in Figures 7.2 and 7.3.

7.3. Mutual Information for Discrete Variables

Consider a channel for which the input is decided by rolling a die with m_x sides. From Section 3.2, we know that if the number of equiprobable

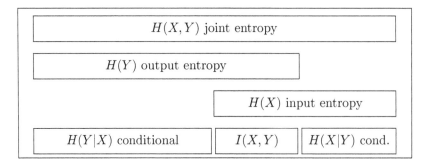

Figure 7.3: The relationship between the input entropy $H(X)$, output entropy $H(Y)$, joint entropy $H(X,Y)$, mutual information $I(X,Y)$, and conditional entropies $H(X|Y)$ and $H(Y|X)$.

input states is m_x then the input entropy is

$$H(X) \quad = \quad \log m_x \text{ bits.} \tag{7.5}$$

For example, if there are $m_x = 8$ equiprobable states $x_1 = 1$, $x_2 = 2$, $x_3 = 3$ and so on, the input entropy is $H(X) = \log 8 = 3$ bits. And if there are $m_\eta = 2$ equiprobable values for the channel noise η, say $\eta_1 = 10$ and $\eta_2 = 20$, then the noise entropy is $H(\eta) = \log 2 = 1$ bit.

Now, if the input is $x_1 = 1$ then the output can be one of two equiprobable values, $y_1 = 1 + 10 = 11$ or $y_2 = 1 + 20 = 21$; and if the input is $x_2 = 2$ then the output can be either $y_3 = 12$ or $y_4 = 22$, and so on. Thus, given eight equiprobable input values and two equiprobable noise values, there are $m_y = 16 \ (= 8 \times 2)$ equiprobable output values. So the output entropy is $H(Y) = \log 16 = 4$ bits. However, some of this entropy comes from noise, so (and this is a crucial point) not all of the output entropy comprises *information about the input*.

In general, the total number m_y of equiprobable output values is $m_y = m_x \times m_\eta$, from which it follows that the output entropy is

$$H(Y) \quad = \quad \log m_x + \log m_\eta \tag{7.6}$$
$$= \quad H(X) + H(\eta) \text{ bits.} \tag{7.7}$$

Because we want to explore channel capacity in terms of channel noise, let us use the symmetry of mutual information and pretend to reverse the direction of data transmission along the channel; that is, rather than using an output value to estimate the input, we use an input value to estimate the corresponding output value. Accordingly, before we are told the input value, we know that the output can be one of 16 values, so our uncertainty about the output value is summarised by its entropy, $H(Y) = 4$ bits.

After we have received an input value (e.g. 1), we know the output must be one of two equiprobable values (i.e. 11 or 21), so our uncertainty about the output is reduced from $H(Y) = 4$ bits to

$$H(Y|X) \quad = \quad H(\eta) \quad = \quad \log 2 \quad = \quad 1 \text{ bit.} \tag{7.8}$$

Note that $H(Y|X)$ is equal to the entropy of the channel noise, $H(\eta)$ (see also Figure 7.1). Equation 7.8 is true for every input; therefore it is true for the average input. Thus, for each input we gain an average of

$$H(Y) - H(Y|X) \quad = \quad 4 - 1 \quad = \quad 3 \text{ bits} \tag{7.9}$$

about the output. According to Equation 7.2, this is the amount of mutual information between X and Y.

In this example, the noise was designed to allow each output to be uniquely associated with one input value, which is why the mutual information equals the input entropy. But notice that this noise meant that we had to use a channel with an output entropy of 4 bits to transmit 3 bits from input to output; if there had been no noise, we could have used this channel to transmit 4 bits. Thus, noise effectively reduces the amount of information that can be transmitted through a channel (see Figure 8.2).

7.4. Mutual Information for Continuous Variables

For continuous variables, the mutual information $I(X,Y)$ between the input X and output Y of a channel determines the number of different input values that can be reliably discriminated from a knowledge of the output. Specifically, the mutual information is the logarithm of the number m of equiprobable input values that can be reliably discriminated from a knowledge of the output values (i.e. $I(X,Y) = \log m$). Because mutual information is symmetric (i.e. $I(X,Y) = I(Y,X)$), m is also the logarithm of the number of equiprobable output values that can be reliably discriminated from a knowledge of the input values.

No Infinity. For a continuous variable Y, its entropy $H(Y)$ includes an infinitely large constant (see Equation 4.8); specifically,

$$H(Y) \quad = \quad \left[\int_y p(y) \log \frac{1}{p(y)} \, dy \right] + \infty \text{ bits}, \tag{7.10}$$

where the integral is the differential entropy $H_{\text{dif}}(Y)$, so that

$$H(Y) \quad = \quad H_{\text{dif}}(Y) + \infty \text{ bits}. \tag{7.11}$$

Similarly, the conditional entropy $H(Y|X)$ can be expressed in terms of the conditional differential entropy $H_{\text{dif}}(Y|X)$ as

$$H(Y|X) \quad = \quad \left[\int_y \int_x p(x,y) \log \frac{1}{p(y|x)} \, dx \, dy \right] + \infty \text{ bits} \quad (7.12)$$

$$= \quad H_{\text{dif}}(Y|X) + \infty \text{ bits}. \quad (7.13)$$

Because the infinite constant in $H(Y)$ and in $H(Y|X)$ is the same, it cancels when we subtract one from the other:

$$I(X,Y) \quad = \quad H(Y) - H(Y|X) \quad (7.14)$$

$$= \quad [H_{\text{dif}}(Y) + \infty] - [H_{\text{dif}}(Y|X) + \infty] \quad (7.15)$$

$$= \quad H_{\text{dif}}(Y) - H_{\text{dif}}(Y|X) \text{ bits}. \quad (7.16)$$

Key point. Even though the entropy of each of the continuous variables X and Y is infinite, the mutual information $I(X,Y)$ between X and Y is finite.

7.5. Mutual Information and Joint Entropy

By definition, the mutual information for continuous variables is

$$I(X,Y) \quad = \quad \int_y \int_x p(x,y) \log \frac{p(x,y)}{p(x)p(y)} \, dx \, dy. \quad (7.17)$$

This can be rewritten as

$$\int_y \int_x p(x,y) \log p(x,y) \, dx \, dy - \int_x p(x) \log p(x) \, dx - \int_y p(y) \log p(y) \, dy,$$

where we can recognise the first, second and third integrals as $-H(X,Y)$, $H(X)$ and $H(Y)$, so that

$$I(X,Y) \quad = \quad H(X) + H(Y) - H(X,Y). \quad (7.18)$$

This result applies to both continuous and discrete variables. We now have three expressions for mutual information,

$$
\begin{aligned}
I(X,Y) &= H(X) - H(X|Y) & (7.19) \\
&= H(Y) - H(Y|X) & (7.20) \\
&= H(X) + H(Y) - H(X,Y) \text{ bits.} & (7.21)
\end{aligned}
$$

From these, a little algebra yields a fourth expression,

$$
I(X,Y) = H(X,Y) - [H(X|Y) + H(Y|X)]. \qquad (7.22)
$$

The mutual information is therefore that portion of the joint entropy $H(X,Y)$ that remains once we have removed the entropy $H(X|Y)$ due to noise in X and the entropy $H(Y|X)$ due to noise in Y.

If we rearrange Equation 7.22 then we obtain

$$
H(X,Y) = I(X,Y) + H(X|Y) + H(Y|X). \qquad (7.23)
$$

Thus, the joint entropy $H(X,Y)$ acts as an 'entropy container' and consists of three disjoint subsets, as shown in Figures 7.2 and 7.3.

> **Key point**. The mutual information is that part of the joint entropy $H(X,Y)$ that remains once we have removed the part $[H(X|Y) + H(Y|X)]$ due to noise.

Mutual Information Cannot Be Negative

If X and Y are independent then knowing the value of Y does not reduce uncertainty regarding the value of X; therefore, in this case $H(X) = H(X|Y)$ so that, from Equation 7.19, $I(X,Y) = 0$. It follows that mutual information is positive unless X and Y are independent, in which case it is zero, so $I(X,Y) \geq 0$.

Chapter 8

Noisy Channels

8.1. The Noisy Channel Coding Theorem

Remarkable as it is, Shannon's source coding theorem ignores the effects of noise. But, as discussed in the previous chapter, noise is everywhere and unavoidable. To study information transmission in a noisy channel, as shown in Figure 8.1, we define the channel capacity as

$$C = \max_{p(x)} I(X, Y) \tag{8.1}$$

$$= \max_{p(x)} \left[H(X) - H(X|Y) \right] \text{ bits/s.} \tag{8.2}$$

In words, the capacity of a noisy channel is given by the input distribution $p(X)$ that maximises the mutual information between the channel inputs and outputs. If there is no noise (i.e. $H(X|Y) = 0$) then this reduces to Equation 6.1, the capacity of a noiseless channel. Recall that $H(X|Y)$ is the conditional entropy which represents the uncertainty that remains regarding the value of X after the value of Y is observed; Shannon referred to it as the *equivocation*. Shannon's *noisy channel coding theorem* is quoted in full here:

> Let a discrete channel have the capacity C [bits/s] and a discrete source the entropy per second $H(X)$. If $H(X) \leq C$ [bits/s] there exists a coding system such that the output of the source can be transmitted over the channel with an arbitrarily small frequency of errors (or an arbitrarily small equivocation $H(X|Y)$). If $H(X) \geq C$ [bits/s] it is possible to encode the source so that the equivocation $H(X|Y)$ is less than $H(X) - C + \epsilon$ where ϵ is arbitrarily small. There is no method of encoding which gives an equivocation $H(X|Y)$ less than $H(X) - C$.

In essence, this theorem says that if a source generates messages with an entropy of $H(X)$ bits/s then an encoding of those messages exists that allows them to be transmitted through a noisy channel (with capacity C bits/s) with an arbitrarily low error rate ϵ (epsilon), provided $H(X) \leq C$ bits/s. However, if the source entropy is larger than the channel capacity (i.e. $H(X) > C$), so that the 'excess source entropy' is $\Delta H(X) = H(X) - C$, then it is not possible for the equivocation $H(X|Y)$ to be less than $\Delta H(X)$.

8.2. Why the Theorem is True

Describing Shannon's proof in detail would require more mathematical tools than we have to hand, so this is a brief summary to give a flavour of his proof. Consider a channel with a fixed amount of channel noise and capacity C. Suppose we have a set of N messages $\mathbf{s}_1, \ldots, \mathbf{s}_N$ which have been encoded to produce channel inputs $\mathbf{x}_1, \ldots, \mathbf{x}_N$ such that the entropy $H(X)$ of these inputs is less than the channel capacity C. Now imagine that we construct a bizarre codebook in which each randomly chosen input $\mathbf{x}_i$ gets interpreted as a fixed, but randomly chosen, output $\mathbf{y}_i$. By chance, some outputs will get assigned the same, or very similar, inputs, and *vice versa*, leading to a degree of cross-talk. Consequently, when we use this codebook to decode outputs, we are bound to misclassify a proportion of them. This proportion is the *error rate* ϵ of the codebook. We then repeat this madness to obtain the average error rate $\bar{\epsilon}$ of all possible codebooks. Shannon proved that, provided $H(X) \leq C$, the average codebook error rate $\bar{\epsilon} \to 0$ as the length n of each input $\mathbf{x}$ approaches infinity, and therefore there must exist at least one codebook with an error rate $\epsilon \to 0$ as $n \to \infty$.

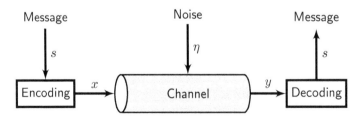

Figure 8.1: The noisy channel. A message is encoded as the input to the channel, which adds noise. The output is decoded to recover the message.

8.3. The Gaussian Channel

If the noise values in a channel are drawn independently from a Gaussian distribution (i.e. $\eta \sim \mathcal{N}(\mu_\eta, v_\eta)$, as defined in Equation 5.7) then this is a *Gaussian channel*.

Because $Y = X + \eta$, if we want $p(Y)$ to be Gaussian we should ensure that $p(X)$ and $p(\eta)$ are both Gaussian, because the sum of two independent Gaussian variables is also Gaussian[28]. So $p(X)$ must be (iid) Gaussian to maximise $H(X)$ (see Section 5.4), which maximises $H(Y)$, which maximises $I(X,Y)$. Thus, if each input, noise and output variable is (iid) Gaussian then the average amount of information communicated per output value is the channel capacity, so that $C - I(X,Y)$ bits/s. This is an informal statement of *Shannon's continuous noisy channel coding theorem for Gaussian channels.*

If the channel input $X \sim \mathcal{N}(\mu_x, v_x)$ then (from Equation 5.8) the differential entropy is

$$H(X) \quad = \quad \tfrac{1}{2}\log 2\pi e v_x \text{ bits/s.} \tag{8.3}$$

Given that the channel noise is iid Gaussian, its entropy $H(\eta)$ is

$$H(Y|X) \quad = \quad \tfrac{1}{2}\log 2\pi e v_\eta \text{ bits/s.} \tag{8.4}$$

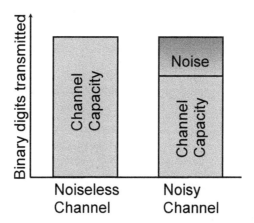

Figure 8.2: The capacity of a noiseless channel is numerically equal to the rate at which it communicates binary digits (for example), whereas the capacity of a noisy channel is limited by the amount of noise in the channel.

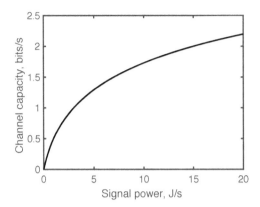

Figure 8.3: Increasing signal power S has diminishing returns on the capacity C of a Gaussian channel (Equation 8.7, with noise power (variance) $N = 1$).

Because the output is the sum $Y = X + \eta$, it is also iid Gaussian with variance $v_y = v_x + v_\eta$, so its entropy is

$$H(Y) = \tfrac{1}{2} \log 2\pi e(v_x + v_\eta) \text{ bits/s.} \tag{8.5}$$

Substituting Equations 8.4 and 8.5 into Equation 7.14 yields

$$I(X,Y) = \tfrac{1}{2} \log (1 + v_x/v_\eta) \text{ bits/s.} \tag{8.6}$$

Because mutual information is maximised when $p(x)$ is Gaussian, this is also the capacity C of a Gaussian channel (see Equation 8.1).

The variance of any signal with a mean of zero is equal to its *power*, which is the rate at which energy is expended per second, and the physical unit of power is joules per second (J/s). Accordingly, the signal power is $S = v_x$ J/s and the noise power is $N = v_\eta$ J/s. This yields Shannon's famous equation for the capacity of a Gaussian channel:

$$C = \tfrac{1}{2} \log (1 + S/N) \text{ bits/s,} \tag{8.7}$$

where S/N is the *signal-to-noise ratio* (SNR), as in Figure 8.3.

> **Key point.** If data are Gaussian with a signal-to-ratio S/N then they can be transmitted at the rate $\tfrac{1}{2} \log (1 + S/N)$ bits/s.

Chapter 9

Rate Distortion Theory

Nature dictates that a signal can be represented either expensively with high fidelity, or cheaply with low fidelity, but it cannot be represented cheaply with high fidelity. Rate distortion theory defines the lowest price that must be paid at every possible value of fidelity. And the only currency Nature accepts as payment is information.

Given a noiseless channel with a fixed capacity C, we can keep increasing the amount of data transmitted and can expect perfect fidelity at the output until the entropy of the input approaches the channel capacity. Up to this point, Shannon's source coding theorem guarantees that the uncertainty, or equivocation, about the input given the output will be close to zero.

However, if we attempt to transmit more data through the channel past this point then the equivocation will increase. Crucially, the transmission rate R remains approximately equal to the channel capacity C, irrespective of how much the input entropy exceeds the channel capacity, as shown in Figure 9.1. Consequently, the increase in equivocation exactly matches the extent to which the input entropy exceeds the channel capacity.

Rate distortion theory[34] expresses the equivocation in terms of the *distortion* D and defines the smallest transmission rate R required for a given level of distortion.

Key point. We can have low distortion at high transmission rates (bits allocated to represent each element), or high distortion at low rates, but we cannot have low distortion at low rates.

9.1. Rate Distortion Theory

Consider a channel with capacity C, for which the input is one element of an n-element vector of iid variables,

$$\mathbf{X} \;=\; (X_1, \ldots, X_n), \tag{9.1}$$

which has entropy $H(\mathbf{X}) = n\,H(X)$. In the simplest case, the channel output is also one element of an n-element vector

$$\hat{\mathbf{X}} \;=\; (\hat{X}_1, \ldots, \hat{X}_n). \tag{9.2}$$

In order to transmit the vector $\mathbf{X}$ through a channel without error, we must transmit at the rate $R = H(X)$ bits/element, so the channel capacity C must be at least R bits/element.

However, if we are willing to tolerate some error or distortion D in the output $\hat{\mathbf{X}}$ then the rate, and therefore the channel capacity C, can be less than $R = H(X)$. As the amount of distortion increases, the uncertainty about the input X given an output $\hat{X}$ also increases, and a convenient measure of this uncertainty is the equivocation $E = H(X|\hat{X})$.

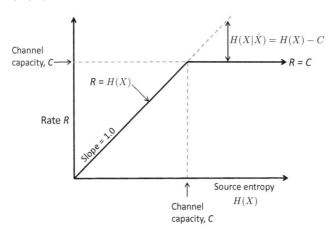

Figure 9.1: Graphical representation of rate distortion theory for a channel with input X, output $\hat{X}$ and capacity C. If $H(X) < C$ then the transmission rate can be as high as $R = H(X)$. If $H(X) > C$ then $R \approx C$, and the dashed diagonal line represents the extent to which the input entropy $H(X)$ exceeds C, which results in an equivocation $H(X|\hat{X}) \geq H(X) - C$.

Rate distortion theory is, in some sense, an extension of the noisy channel coding theorem, which places a lower bound on the equivocation,

$$H(X|\hat{X}) \geq H(X) - C \text{ bits,} \tag{9.3}$$

as shown in Figure 9.1. Shannon succinctly summarised the implication of this bound as follows[35]:

> If an attempt is made to transmit at a higher rate than C, say $C + E$, then there will necessarily be an equivocation equal to or greater than the excess E. Nature takes payment by requiring just that much uncertainty.

Notation. For the sake of brevity, we avoid the verbal somersaults required to express the limiting behaviour of information rates in this chapter. Accordingly, we will sometimes take the liberty of replacing phrases such as '$R \to C$ as $n \to \infty$' with simply '$R = C$'.

The Rate Distortion Function

The *rate distortion function* $R(D)$ is defined as the smallest number of bits or rate R that must be allocated to represent X as a distorted version $\hat{X}$ for a given level of distortion D, which is defined by

$$D = \mathrm{E}[d(\mathbf{X}, \hat{\mathbf{X}})] \tag{9.4}$$

$$= \sum_{\mathbf{x}} p(\mathbf{x}) d(\mathbf{x}, \hat{\mathbf{x}}), \tag{9.5}$$

where $d(\mathbf{x}, \hat{\mathbf{x}}) = \frac{1}{n} \sum_i d(x_i, \hat{x}_i)$ and $d(x_i, \hat{x}_i)$ is a *distortion measure*, such as the squared difference $d(x_i, \hat{x}_i) = (x_i - \hat{x}_i)^2$.

Rate distortion theory also defines the *distortion rate function* $D(R)$ as the smallest distortion D that is consistent with a given rate R.

> **Key point.** A rate distortion function $R(D)$ specifies the smallest number of bits or rate R required to represent a variable X as a distorted version $\hat{X}$ with a level of distortion no greater than D.

9.2. The Binary Rate Distortion Function

Consider a binary vector **x**, where the probability of each element being 1 is p. If the distortion measure is

$$d(x, \hat{x}) \;=\; \begin{cases} 0 & \text{if } x = \hat{x}, \\ 1 & \text{if } x \neq \hat{x}, \end{cases} \tag{9.6}$$

then it can be shown that the binary rate distortion function is

$$R(D) = \begin{cases} H(p) - H(D) \text{ bits} & \text{if } 0 \leq D \leq \min\{p, 1-p\}, \\ 0 \text{ bits} & \text{if } D > \min\{p, 1-p\}, \end{cases} \tag{9.7}$$

as shown in Figure 9.2 for $p = 0.5$. Notice that the rate is $R(D) = 1$ bit when $D = 0$, as we would expect from a noiseless binary variable.

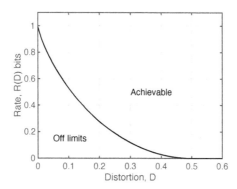

Figure 9.2: Rate distortion function for a binary source with $p = 0.5$ (Equation 9.7). Only the region above the curve corresponds to (R, D) values that can be achieved.

9.3. The Gaussian Rate Distortion Function

Consider a vector $\mathbf{x}$ of n elements x, each of which is drawn from a Gaussian distribution $\mathcal{N}(0, \sigma^2)$. If the distortion measure is $d(x_i, \hat{x}_i) = (x_i - \hat{x}_i)^2$ then

$$d(\mathbf{x}, \hat{\mathbf{x}}) \quad = \quad \frac{1}{n} \sum_{i=1}^{n} (x_i - \hat{x}_i)^2. \tag{9.8}$$

It can be shown that if the source has variance σ^2 then the rate distortion function is

$$R(D) \quad = \quad \begin{cases} \frac{1}{2} \log \frac{\sigma^2}{D} & \text{if } 0 \le D \le \sigma^2, \\ 0 & \text{if } D > \sigma^2. \end{cases} \tag{9.9}$$

For example, if $\sigma^2 = 1$ then $R(D) = \frac{1}{2} \log \frac{1}{D}$ bits, as shown in Figure 9.3. Notice that $R(D) \to \infty$ bits as $D \to 0$, as we would expect given that the exact value of a real variable conveys an infinite amount of information (see Section 4.1).

Rearranging Equation 9.9 yields the distortion rate function

$$D(R) \quad = \quad \sigma^2 / 2^{2R}. \tag{9.10}$$

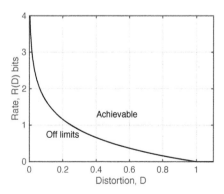

Figure 9.3: Rate distortion function for a Gaussian source with variance $\sigma^2 = 1$ (Equation 9.9). Only the region above the curve corresponds to (R, D) values that can be achieved.

This implies that each extra bit added to the rate R decreases the mean distortion by a factor of $2^2 = 4$. For example, if the encoding function yields $\hat{\mathbf{x}}$ such that each element of $\hat{\mathbf{x}}$ has entropy $R = 1$ bit then the smallest mean squared error is $D(R) = 0.25\sigma^2$.

9.4. Image Compression Example

Consider a picture $\mathbf{x} = (x_1, x_2, \ldots, x_n)$ with n pixels in which each pixel grey-level (brightness) is one of 64 values, as in Figure 9.4a. For simplicity, we assume that the grey-levels in $\mathbf{x}$ are iid, so we can estimate the entropy of $\mathbf{x}$ from the distribution of grey-levels (Figure 9.4b) as

$$H(x) \quad = \quad 5.845 \text{ bits.} \tag{9.11}$$

(This is different from the entropy quoted in Section 6.3 because we have used a different degree of quantisation here.) The variance of the grey-levels $\mathbf{x}$ shown in Figure 9.4a is $\sigma^2 = 258$. By quantising (encoding) the 64 grey-levels in $\mathbf{x}$ into 4 grey-levels, we obtain the distorted image $\hat{\mathbf{x}}$ in Figure 9.4c.

Briefly, the lossy compression implemented by the quantisation from $\mathbf{x}$ to $\hat{\mathbf{x}}$ was achieved as follows. Each pixel in $\mathbf{x}$ with a grey-level between 1 and 16 was replaced with a mid-point grey-level of 8 in $\hat{\mathbf{x}}$, each pixel in $\mathbf{x}$ with a grey-level between 17 and 32 was replaced with a mid-point grey-level of 24 in $\hat{\mathbf{x}}$, and similarly for the third and fourth ranges. The proportion of pixels within each of these 4 ranges is shown in Figure 9.4d.

For a given image $\mathbf{x}$ and its distorted version $\hat{\mathbf{x}}$, the rate is

$$R \quad = \quad I(x; \hat{x}) \tag{9.12}$$
$$= \quad H(\hat{x}) - H(\hat{x}|x) \text{ bits.} \tag{9.13}$$

However, because in this example the mapping from $\mathbf{x}$ to $\hat{\mathbf{x}}$ is deterministic, it follows that $H(\hat{x}|x) = 0$, and therefore the rate is $R = H(\hat{x})$ bits. From the distribution $p(\hat{x})$ in Figure 9.4d (again

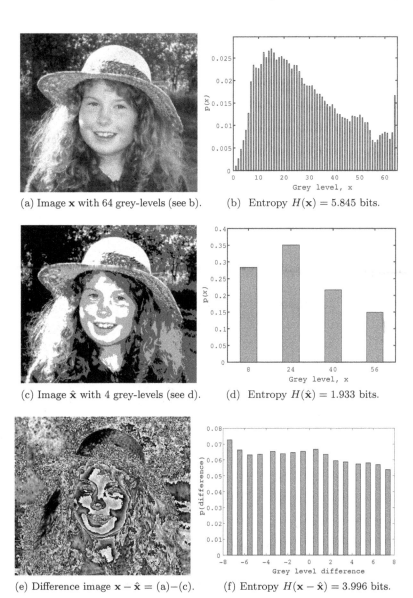

(a) Image **x** with 64 grey-levels (see b).

(b) Entropy $H(\mathbf{x}) = 5.845$ bits.

(c) Image $\hat{\mathbf{x}}$ with 4 grey-levels (see d).

(d) Entropy $H(\hat{\mathbf{x}}) = 1.933$ bits.

(e) Difference image $\mathbf{x} - \hat{\mathbf{x}} = $ (a)−(c).

(f) Entropy $H(\mathbf{x} - \hat{\mathbf{x}}) = 3.996$ bits.

Figure 9.4: Lossy compression of (a) yields (c).
(a) Image **x** with 64 grey-levels.
(b) The distribution of grey-levels in (a) with entropy $H(x) = 5.845$ bits.
(c) Compressed version $\hat{\mathbf{x}}$ of **x** with 4 grey-levels (codewords).
(d) Distribution of grey-levels (codewords) in (c) with $H(\hat{x}) = 1.933$ bits.
(e) Difference $\mathbf{x} - \hat{\mathbf{x}}$ between the images in (a) and (c).
(f) Distribution of grey-levels in (e) with entropy $H(\mathbf{x} - \hat{\mathbf{x}}) = 3.996$ bits.

assuming iid grey-levels), this evaluates to

$$R = \sum_{i=1}^{4} p(\hat{x}_i) \log \frac{1}{p(\hat{x}_i)} = 1.933 \text{ bits}. \qquad (9.14)$$

Using the mean squared distortion measure (Equation 9.8), the distortion imposed on $\mathbf{x}$ in (a) to obtain $\hat{\mathbf{x}}$ in (c) is the variance of the 'difference image' (a) − (c) = $\mathbf{x} - \hat{\mathbf{x}}$ shown in Figure 9.4e, which is

$$d(\mathbf{x}, \hat{\mathbf{x}}) = 20.97. \qquad (9.15)$$

We assume $D = 20.97$ for convenience below.

How Good is the Compression?

To compare the measured value of $d(\mathbf{x}, \hat{\mathbf{x}})$ and R values with values that could be obtained under ideal (i.e. Gaussian) conditions, we can assume that 1) the distributions $p(\hat{x})$ and $p(x)$ are Gaussian and, therefore, 2) the distribution of errors $x - \hat{x}$ is Gaussian, and 3) the expected

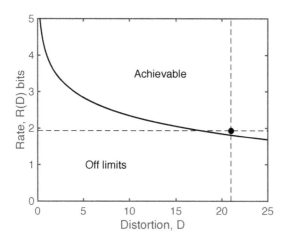

Figure 9.5: Rate distortion function $R(D)$ for Figure 9.4, assuming the distributions are Gaussian (Equation 9.9 with $\sigma^2 = 258$). The distortion imposed by quantising $\mathbf{x}$ in Figure 9.4a into $\hat{\mathbf{x}}$ in Figure 9.4c is $D = 20.97$, and the rate for this quantised image is $R = 1.933$ bits, indicated by the black dot. For comparison, under ideal (i.e. Gaussian) conditions, the minimum rate at $D = 20.97$ would be $R(D) = 1.810$ bits, indicated by the intersection of the vertical dashed line with the rate distortion function.

distortion equals the measured distortion, $D = d(\mathbf{x}, \hat{\mathbf{x}}) = 20.97$. So, if the grey-levels were Gaussian with variance $\sigma^2 = 258$ then the minimal rate $R(D)$ that could be achieved with the distortion $D = 20.97$ would be given by Equation 9.9 as

$$R(D) \;=\; \tfrac{1}{2} \log\left(\sigma^2/D\right) \;=\; \tfrac{1}{2} \log\left(258/20.97\right) \;=\; 1.810 \text{ bits}. \quad (9.16)$$

However, the lossy compression used here, which maps $\mathbf{x}$ to $\hat{\mathbf{x}}$, has a rate of $R = I(x; \hat{x}) = 1.933$ bits. As shown in Figure 9.5, this is only a little larger than the optimal rate of $R(D) = 1.810$ bits given the measured distortion in $\hat{\mathbf{x}}$ (Figure 9.4e) of $D = 20.97$. This near-optimality of the measured value of $R = 1.933$ bits is unsurprising because the distributions $p(x)$ and $p(x - \hat{x})$ are (very loosely speaking) approximately Gaussian.

Similarly, using these Gaussian assumptions, Equation 9.10 provides the smallest distortion that could be achieved with the measured values of R and σ^2,

$$D(R) \;=\; \sigma^2/2^{2R} \;=\; 258/2^{2 \times 1.933} \;=\; 17.69. \quad (9.17)$$

In contrast, the measured value of distortion is $D = 20.97$, which is only about 20% larger than its theoretical minimum value of $D(R) = 17.69$.

In practice, and as noted by Shannon[34], naive coding schemes can provide reasonably efficient codes. However, in the age of the internet, even the small difference between reasonably efficient codes and codes that approach the Shannon limit defined by the rate distortion function $R(D)$ can amount to millions of dollars. After several false starts, and a general belief that Shannon efficient codes don't exist, *Gallager codes* finally emerged as the modern standard used in phone and satellite communication systems; Gallager codes are efficient inasmuch as they are very close to the Shannon limit. Efficiency clearly matters for transmission in Earth-bound systems, but it is absolutely essential for receiving data from NASA's Mars Rover, which transmits to Earth at the dismal rate of 800 binary digits/s. For comparison, a typical wifi system communicates at about 50 million binary digits/s.

Whereas information theory assumes an ideal world in which channel capacity is sufficient to transmit messages without error (in principle), rate distortion theory relies on the more realistic assumption that channel capacity is never sufficient, and therefore some degree of error must be tolerated. Even though rate distortion theory does not provide a 'free lunch', in terms of information and distortion it does specify the lowest possible information price that must be paid for data with a given level of distortion.

Chapter 10

Transfer Entropy

Transfer entropy[31] represents one of the few theoretical advances since Shannon's original paper of 1948. It was devised to harness information theory to measure the *causal relations* between variables. Accordingly, transfer entropy is based on the following observation:

> If a change in the value of a *causal variable* X induces changes in an *affected variable* Y then each change in X must precede the corresponding changes in Y.

A unique feature of transfer entropy is that it can detect the influence of the current value of X on future values of Y, irrespective of the nature of that dependence (i.e. even if the dependence is nonlinear). This contrasts with measures such as *Granger causality*[36], which can detect only linear dependences between X and Y. Related measures are *directed information*[21] and *compression complexity causality*[17].

Transfer entropy has been used in a variety of applications, including studies of gradient-climbing bacteria[22], bat behaviour[25] and climate change[41], ecohydrology[30], earthquake prediction[9], neurodynamics[39] and neuroscience[40], electroencephalogram (EEG) analysis[7], and biomedical time series analysis[19].

10.1. Transfer Entropy

The uncertainty about (entropy of) the current value y_t of the affected variable Y given past values y_{past} of Y is the conditional entropy

$$\text{uncertainty in } y_t \text{ given } y_{\text{past}} = H(y_t|y_{\text{past}}) \text{ bits.} \qquad (10.1)$$

Similarly, the amount of uncertainty about the current value y_t given past values of both X and Y is the conditional entropy

$$\text{uncertainty in } y_t \text{ given } y_\text{past} \text{ and } x_\text{past} = H(y_t|y_\text{past}, x_\text{past}) \text{ bits.} \quad (10.2)$$

Taking account of past values of both X and Y usually *decreases* uncertainty about y_t, which yields the transfer entropy:

$$
\begin{aligned}
\text{transfer entropy} \quad &= \quad [\text{uncertainty in } y_t \text{ given } y_\text{past}] \\
&\quad - [\text{uncertainty in } y_t \text{ given } y_\text{past} \text{ and } x_\text{past}] \\
&= \quad \text{changes in } y_t \text{ due only to } x_\text{past}.
\end{aligned}
$$

From Equations 10.1 and 10.2, this can be written as

$$T_{x_\text{past} \to y_t} \quad = \quad H(y_t|y_\text{past}) - H(y_t|y_\text{past}, x_\text{past}) \text{ bits,} \quad (10.3)$$

as shown in Figures 10.1 and 10.2.

To take a slightly different perspective, because decreasing the uncertainty about the current value y_t is equivalent to increasing the amount of information about y_t, it follows that transfer entropy is the extra information that x_past provides about y_t, over and above the

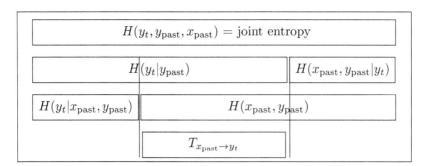

Figure 10.1: Transfer entropy is the information about y_t provided by x_past that is not also provided by y_past. The vertical lines indicate how transfer entropy equals mutual information, $T_{x_\text{past} \to y_t} = I(y_t; x_\text{past}|y_\text{past})$, which can be obtained as either the difference $H(y_t|y_\text{past}) - H(y_t|x_\text{past}, y_\text{past})$ or the difference $H(x_\text{past}, y_\text{past}) - H(x_\text{past}, y_\text{past}|y_t)$.

information that y_{past} provides about y_t:

$$T_{x_{\text{past}} \to y_t} \quad = \quad I(y_t; x_{\text{past}} | y_{\text{past}}) \tag{10.4}$$

$$= \quad I(y_t; y_{\text{past}}, x_{\text{past}}) - I(y_t; y_{\text{past}}) \text{ bits.} \tag{10.5}$$

> **Key point.** Given variables X and Y, where past values x_{past} of X affect the current value y_t of Y, the transfer entropy $T_{x_{\text{past}} \to y_t}$ is the average information that x_{past} provides about y_t, over and above the information that y_{past} itself provides about y_t.

To be more precise about what we mean by the past, transfer entropy can be defined in terms of the temporal variables[24] k and n:

$$T_{x_{\text{past}} \to y_t}(k, n) = I\big(y_t; (x_{t-n}, \ldots, x_{t-1}) \big| (y_{t-k}, \ldots, y_{t-1})\big). \tag{10.6}$$

However, it is common practice to set $n=k=0$, as in the examples below.

Transfer Entropy and Causation

The simple observation on the first page of this chapter represents a *necessary, but not sufficient,* condition for establishing causality. For example, if changes in X precede corresponding changes in Y then this may be because X causes Y to change, or it may be because both X

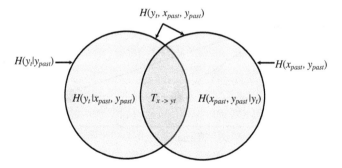

Figure 10.2: Venn diagram of transfer entropy. Each circle represents the entropy of one or more variables, and the total area of the three labelled regions represents the joint entropy $H(y_t, x_{\text{past}}, y_{\text{past}})$.

and Y are affected by a third variable, Z. Specifically, if Z affects X before it affects Y then this can give the false impression that X affects Y, as shown in Figure 10.3. Having acknowledged this problem, we can proceed by defining transfer entropy as the extent to which past values of X are related to the current value of Y.

10.2. The Pendulum

A reasonably intuitive example of transfer entropy is provided by the pendulum. Accordingly, consider a pendulum with height y_t at time t. The momentum of the pendulum ensures that the height at all future times could be calculated exactly. Instead of considering all past and future times, we can simplify matters by restricting attention to pairs of consecutive time steps. In this case, the mutual information between y_{t-1} and y_t is

$$I(y_t; y_{t-1}) \quad = \quad H(y_t) - H(y_t|y_{t-1}) \text{ bits}, \qquad (10.7)$$

where $H(y_t|y_{t-1}) = H(\eta_y)$ is a conditional entropy, which could correspond to the noise introduced by air molecules (for example). However, if the pendulum is given a nudge x_{t-1} by an external force X then y_t depends on both x_{t-1} and y_{t-1}, so both x_{t-1} and y_{t-1} provide information about y_t. In this case, the mutual information between y_t

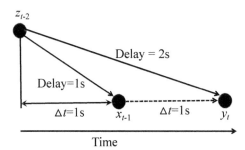

Figure 10.3: A variable z_{t-2} at time $t - 2$ takes $\Delta t = 1$ second to affect X at x_{t-1}, and takes $2\Delta t = 2$ seconds to affect Y at y_t, so the states of x_{t-1} and y_t are correlated. If only X and Y can be observed then this can give the false impression that x_{t-1} affects y_t, as indicated by the dashed arrow.

and the pair x_{t-1} and y_{t-1} is

$$I(y_t; y_{t-1}, x_{t-1}) \quad = \quad H(y_t) - H(y_t|y_{t-1}, x_{t-1}) \text{ bits.} \quad (10.8)$$

Notice that if the pendulum is nudged with an external force x_{t-1} then

$$I(y_t; x_{t-1}, y_{t-1}) \quad > \quad I(y_t; y_{t-1}) \text{ bits.} \quad (10.9)$$

From Equation 10.5, the transfer entropy is

$$T_{x_{t-1} \to y_t} \quad = \quad I(y_t; y_{t-1}, x_{t-1}) - I(y_t, y_{t-1}) \text{ bits.} \quad (10.10)$$

This definition is usually written in terms of conditional entropy by substituting Equations 10.7 and 10.8 into Equation 10.10, which yields

$$T_{x_{t-1} \to y_t} \quad = \quad H(y_t|y_{t-1}) - H(y_t|x_{t-1}, y_{t-1}) \text{ bits.} \quad (10.11)$$

Similarly, the information transferred from y_{t-1} to x_t is

$$T_{y_{t-1} \to x_t} \quad = \quad H(x_t|x_{t-1}) - H(x_t|x_{t-1}, y_{t-1}) \text{ bits.} \quad (10.12)$$

A crucial feature of transfer entropy is that, unlike mutual information, it is not symmetric: if the past x_{t-1} affects the present y_t but not vice versa, it follows that $T_{x_{t-1} \to y_t} > 0$, whereas $T_{y_t \to x_{t-1}} = 0$.

10.3. Numerical Example

Consider a process with causal variable X and affected variable Y:

$$x_t \quad = \quad b_x x_{t-1} + \eta_{x,t-1}, \quad (10.13)$$

$$y_t \quad = \quad b_y y_{t-1} + \lambda x_{t-1} + \eta_{y,t-1}, \quad (10.14)$$

where the noise terms $\eta_{x,t-1}$ and $\eta_{y,t-1}$ have Gaussian distributions, $\eta_{x,t-1} \sim \mathcal{N}(0, \sigma_x^2)$ and $\eta_{y,t-1} \sim \mathcal{N}(0, \sigma_y^2)$. Notice that the value x_{t-1} of the causal variable X induces changes in the affected variable Y at all times after $t-1$, but that Y has no effect on X.

The values in Equations 10.13 and 10.14 are $b_x = 0.8$, $b_y = 0.4$, $\sigma_x = 0.2^{1/2}$, $\sigma_y = 0.2^{1/2}$ and $\lambda = [0, 1]$, as in Edinburgh et al (2021)[6]. A

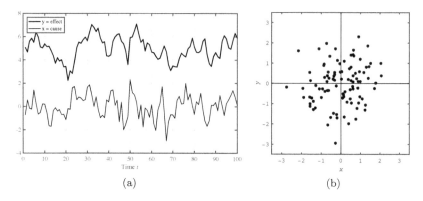

Figure 10.4: a) A causal or source variable X (lower curve, Equation 10.13) and an affected or sink variable Y (upper curve, Equation 10.14), with $\lambda = 0.9$ (upper curve has been shifted vertically for display purposes). b) Scatterplot of 100 X and Y values. The correlation based on 10^5 samples is $\rho = 0.212$.

sample of 100 values of X and Y (with $\lambda = 0.9$) is plotted in Figure 10.4a, and the scatterplot of X and Y is shown in Figure 10.4b.

Using $n = 10^5$ samples from Equations 10.13 and 10.14, the transfer entropy $T_{x_{t-1} \to y_t}$ (the entropy transferred from x_{t-1} to y_t) is

$$T_{x_{t-1} \to y_t} \quad = \quad 0.331 \text{ bits.} \tag{10.15}$$

For this particular linear process, there is an analytical expression for the transfer entropy (see Edinburgh $et\ al$, 2021[6]), which yields

$$T_{x_{t-1} \to y_t} \quad = \quad 0.327 \text{ bits,} \tag{10.16}$$

similar to the value estimated from data in Equation 10.15.

Conversely, the entropy transferred from y_{t-1} to x_t is defined in Equation 10.12. However, according to Equations 10.13 and 10.14, the value of x_t does not depend on y_{t-1}, so

$$H(x_t|x_{t-1}) \quad = \quad H(x_t|x_{t-1}, y_{t-1}) \text{ bits.} \tag{10.17}$$

Substituting this into Equation 10.12 yields $T_{y_{t-1} \to x_t} = 0$ bits. As predicted, the estimated transfer entropy for the data above was found to be close to zero, $T_{y_{t-1} \to x_t} = 0.001$ bits.

Further Reading

Applebaum, D. (2008)[1]. *Probability and Information: An Integrated Approach.* A thorough introduction to information theory, which strikes a good balance between intuitive and technical explanations.

Avery, J. (2012)[2]. *Information Theory and Evolution.* An engaging account of how information theory is relevant to a wide range of natural and constructed systems, including evolution, physics, culture and genetics. Includes interesting background stories on the development of ideas within these different disciplines.

Baeyer, H. V. (2005)[3]. *Information: The New Language of Science.* Erudite, wide-ranging and insightful account of information theory. Contains no equations, which makes it very readable.

Cover, T. and Thomas, J. (1991)[5]. *Elements of Information Theory.* Comprehensive and highly technical, with historical notes and an equation summary at the end of each chapter.

Ghahramani, Z. (2002). *Information Theory.* In *Encyclopedia of Cognitive Science.* An excellent, brief overview of information theory.

Gibson, J. D. (2014)[12]. *Information Theory and Rate Distortion Theory for Communications and Compression.* A short (115 pages) introduction to information theory and rate distortion theory that is both formal and reasonably accessible, with an emphasis on key theorems and proofs.

Gleick, J. (2012)[13]. *The Information.* An informal introduction to the history of ideas and people associated with information theory.

Guizzo, E. M. (2003)[14]. *The Essential Message: Claude Shannon and the Making of Information Theory.* Master's Thesis, Massachusetts Institute of Technology. One of the few accounts of Shannon's role in the development of information theory. See `http://dspace.mit.edu/bitstream/handle/1721.1/39429/54526133.pdf`.

MacKay, D. J. C. (2003)[20]. *Information Theory, Inference, and Learning Algorithms.* The modern classic on information theory. A very readable text that roams far and wide over many topics. The book's website (below) also has a link to an excellent series of video lectures by MacKay. Available free online at `http://www.inference.phy.cam.ac.uk/mackay/itila/`.

Pierce, J. R. (1980)[27]. *An Introduction to Information Theory: Symbols, Signals and Noise*, Second Edition. Pierce writes with an informal, tutorial style of writing, but does not flinch from presenting the fundamental theorems of information theory. This book provides a good balance between words and equations.

Reza, F. M. (1961)[28]. *An Introduction to Information Theory.* A comprehensive and mathematically rigorous book; it should be read only after first reading Pierce's more informal text.

Shannon, C. E. and Weaver, W. (1949)[35]. *The Mathematical Theory of Communication.* A surprisingly accessible book, written in an era when information theory was relatively unknown.

Shannon, C. E. (1959)[34]. *Coding theorems for a discrete source with a fidelity criterion.* Shannon's 22-page paper on rate distortion theory.

Stone, J. V. (2022)[37]. *Information Theory: A Tutorial Introduction*, Second Edition. Information theory explained at a more leisurely pace than this text.

The Bit Player is a fine documentary of Shannon's life and works (available at cinema special showings).

Fritterin' Away Genius. Tim Harford's podcast provides insight into Shannon's playful personality. Available at `https://omny.fm/shows/cautionary-tales-with-tim-harford/fritterin-away-genius`.

Appendix A

Glossary

average The average, mean or expected value of n values of a variable X is $\bar{x} = \frac{1}{n}\sum_{j=1}^{n} x_j$.

binary digit A digit whose value can be either 0 or 1.

binary number A number that consists of binary digits (e.g. 1001).

bit A fundamental unit of information, often confused with a binary digit (see Section 2.2). A bit is exactly the amount of information required to choose from one of two equally probable alternatives.

byte An ordered set of 8 binary digits.

capacity The capacity of a communication channel is the maximum rate at which it can communicate information from its input to its output. Capacity can be specified in terms of either information communicated per unit time (e.g. bits/s), or information communicated per symbol (e.g. bits/symbol).

channel A conduit for communicating data from one point (its input) to another (its output).

codebook The set of codewords produced by a given encoder.

codeword The form x in which each symbol s in a message is encoded before transmission.

conditional probability The probability that the value of one random variable Y has the value y given that the value of another random variable X has the value x, written as $p(Y = y|X = x)$ or $p(y|x)$.

conditional entropy The average uncertainty regarding the value of a random variable Y when the value of another random variable X is known, $H(Y|X) = \mathrm{E}[\log(1/p(y|x))]$ bits.

continuous Whereas a discrete variable adopts a discrete number of values, a continuous variable can adopt any value (e.g. a decimal).

differential entropy The expected value of the surprisal $\log(1/p(x))$ of a continuous random variable, $\mathrm{E}[\log(1/p(x))]$.

discrete Elements of a set that are clearly separated from each other, such as a list of integers, are called discrete.

encoding Before a message is transmitted, it is encoded as an input sequence. Ideally, the encoding process ensures that each element of the encoded message conveys as much information as possible.

equivocation Average uncertainty in the value of the channel input x when the output y is known, measured as conditional entropy $H(X|Y)$.

entropy A measure of a variable's overall variability. Formally, the entropy of a random variable is the average amount of Shannon information, uncertainty or surprisal associated with *each value* of that variable. The entropy of a discrete iid variable X that has m possible values x_i with probabilities $p(x_i)$ is

$$H(X) \quad = \quad \sum_{i=1}^{N} p(x_i) \log_2 \frac{1}{p(x_i)} \text{ bits.} \qquad \text{(A.1)}$$

If values of x are not iid then the entropy is less than $H(X)$.

expected value See average.

histogram If we count the number of times a discrete variable adopts each of a number of values then the resultant set of counts defines a histogram.

iid If values are chosen independently (i.e. 'at random') from a single probability distribution then they are said to be iid (*independent and identically distributed*). All variables in this text are assumed to be iid unless stated otherwise.

independence If two variables X and Y are independent then the value x of X provides no information regarding the value y of Y, and *vice versa*.

information The amount of information conveyed by a discrete iid variable X that takes value x is $h(x) = \log(1/p(x))$. The average amount of information conveyed by each value of X is its entropy $H(X) = \sum p(x_i) \log(1/p(x_i)) = \mathrm{E}[\log(1/p(x))]$ bits.

joint probability The probability that two or more quantities simultaneously adopt specified values. For example, the probability that one die yields $x_3 = 3$ and another die yields $y_4 = 4$ is the joint probability $p(x_3, y_4) = 1/36$. When considered over all values of X and Y, these probabilities define a *joint probability distribution* $p(X, Y)$.

joint entropy The entropy of a joint probability distribution $p(X, Y)$ is $\mathrm{E}[\log(1/p(x, y))]$ bits per pair.

law of large numbers Given a variable X with mean μ, the mean $\bar{x}$ of a sample of n values of X converges to μ as the number of values in that sample approaches infinity; that is, $\bar{x} \to \mu$ as $n \to \infty$.

logarithm Given a positive number x, the logarithm to base a of x, written as $\log_a x$, is the power to which we have to raise a in order to get x. See Section 2.1.

mean See average.

message A sequence of symbols or values, represented as bold **s** or non-bold s according to context.

mutual information The reduction in uncertainty $I(Y, X)$ regarding the value of one variable Y induced by knowing the value of another variable X. Mutual information is symmetric, so $I(X, Y) = I(Y, X)$.

noise The random 'jitter' that is part of a measured quantity.

outcome In this text, the term outcome refers to a single instance of a physical outcome, such as the pair of numbers showing after a pair of dice is thrown. In terms of random variables, an outcome is the result of a single experiment.

outcome value In this text, the term outcome value refers to the numerical value assigned to a single physical outcome. For example, if a pair of dice is thrown then the outcome (x_1, x_2) comprises two numbers, and the outcome value can be defined as the sum of these two numbers, $x = x_1 + x_2$. In terms of the random variable X, the outcome value is the numerical value assigned to the outcome (x_1, x_2), written as $x = X(x_1, x_2)$.

probability There are many definitions of probability. The two main ones are (using a coin as an example): (1) Bayesian – an observer's estimate of the probability that a coin will land heads up is based on all the information the observer has, including the proportion of times it was observed to land heads up in the past; (2) frequentist – the probability that a coin will land heads up is given by the proportion of times it has landed heads up in the past, measured over many flips.

probability density function (pdf) The probability density function $p(X)$ of a continuous random variable X defines the probability density for each value of X. Loosely speaking, the probability that $X = x$ can be considered as the probability density $p(x)$.

probability distribution The probability distribution $p(X)$ of a discrete random variable X defines the probability of each value of X. The probability that $X = x$ is $p(X = x)$ or, more succinctly, $p(x)$. This is called a *probability mass function* (pmf) in some texts.

random variable The concept of a random variable X can be understood from a simple example, such as throwing a pair of dice. Each physical outcome is a pair of numbers (x_a, x_b), with an outcome value x (e.g. $x = x_a + x_b$) which is the value of the random variable, written as $X = x$. The probability of each outcome value x_i is defined by a probability distribution $p(X) = \{p(x_1), p(x_2), \dots\}$.

rate In information theory, this refers to the rate R at which information is transmitted from the input X to the output Y of a channel, $R = H(X) - H(X|Y)$ bits/s, which cannot exceed the channel capacity C. In rate distortion theory, the output $\hat{X}$ is a distorted version of X, and the rate R is the entropy $H(\hat{X})$ of $\hat{X}$, which is the number of bits allocated to represent element X of a signal $\mathbf{X} = (X_1, \ldots, X_n)$.

rate distortion function The smallest number of bits or rate R that must be allocated to represent X as a distorted version $\hat{X}$ for a given level of distortion D.

rate distortion theory A theory that provides a theoretical bound on the information required to represent a signal with a given level of distortion.

redundancy Given an ordered set of values of a variable (e.g. in an image or sound), if a value can be obtained from knowledge of other values then it is redundant.

standard deviation The square root σ of the variance of a variable.

surprisal For a random variable X with value x that occurs with probability $p(x)$, the amount of information provided by an observation of x is its surprisal $h(x) = \log(1/p(x))$ bits.

theorem A mathematical statement that has been proven to be true.

transfer entropy Given variables X and Y, the transfer entropy $T_{x_{\text{past}} \to y_t}$ is the average information that past values x_{past} provide about the current value y_t, over and above the information that y_{past} provides about y_t.

transmission rate See rate.

uncertainty In this text, uncertainty refers to the surprisal or average surprisal (entropy) of a variable.

variance The variance is a measure of how 'spread out' the values of a variable are. Given a sample of n values of a variable X with a sample mean of $\bar{x}$, the estimated variance $\hat{v}_x$ of X is

$$\hat{v}_x = \frac{1}{n} \sum_{j=1}^{n} (x_j - \bar{x})^2.$$

Appendix B

Key Equations

Entropy

$$H(X) = \sum_{i=1}^{N} p(x_i) \log \frac{1}{p(x_i)} \tag{B.1}$$

$$H_{\text{dif}}(X) - \int_x p(x) \log \frac{1}{p(x)} \, dx \tag{B.2}$$

Joint entropy

$$H(X,Y) = \sum_{i=1}^{m_x} \sum_{j=1}^{m_y} p(x_i, y_j) \log \frac{1}{p(x_i, y_j)} \tag{B.3}$$

$$H_{\text{dif}}(X,Y) = \int_x \int_y p(x, y) \log \frac{1}{p(x, y)} \, dy \, dx \tag{B.4}$$

$$H(X,Y) = I(X,Y) + H(X|Y) + H(Y|X) \tag{B.5}$$

Conditional Entropy

$$H(Y|X) = \sum_{i=1}^{m_x} \sum_{j=1}^{m_y} p(x_i, y_j) \log \frac{1}{p(y_j|x_i)} \tag{B.6}$$

$$H(X|Y) = \sum_{i=1}^{m_x} \sum_{j=1}^{m_y} p(x_i, y_j) \log \frac{1}{p(x_i|y_j)} \tag{B.7}$$

$$H_{\text{dif}}(X|Y) = \int_y \int_x p(x, y) \log \frac{1}{p(x|y)} \, dx \, dy \tag{B.8}$$

$$H_{\text{dif}}(Y|X) = \int_y \int_x p(x, y) \log \frac{1}{p(y|x)} \, dx \, dy \tag{B.9}$$

$$H(X|Y) = H(X,Y) - H(Y) \tag{B.10}$$

$$H(Y|X) = H(X,Y) - H(X) \tag{B.11}$$

Mutual Information

$$I(X,Y) = \sum_{i=1}^{m_x} \sum_{j=1}^{m_y} p(x_i, y_j) \log \frac{p(x_i, y_j)}{p(x_i)p(y_j)} \tag{B.12}$$

$$I(X,Y) = \int_y \int_x p(x,y) \log \frac{p(x,y)}{p(x)p(y)} \, dx \, dy \tag{B.13}$$

$$
\begin{aligned}
I(X,Y) &= H(X) + H(Y) - H(X,Y) & \text{(B.14)}\\
&= H(X) - H(X|Y) & \text{(B.15)}\\
&= H(Y) - H(Y|X) & \text{(B.16)}\\
&= H(X,Y) - [H(X|Y) + H(Y|X)] & \text{(B.17)}
\end{aligned}
$$

Channel Capacity

$$C = \max_{p(X)} I(X,Y) \text{ bits/s} \tag{B.18}$$

If the channel input X has variance S, the noise η has variance N, and both X and η are iid Gaussian variables then $I(X,Y) = C$, and

$$C = \frac{1}{2} \log \left(1 + \frac{S}{N}\right) \text{ bits/s} \tag{B.19}$$

Rate Distortion Function
The *rate distortion function* $R(D)$ is the smallest number of bits or rate R that must be allocated to represent X as a distorted version $\hat{X}$ with a level of distortion no greater than D:

$$R(D) = \min_{p(\hat{x}|x): \, \mathrm{E}[d(x,\hat{x})] \leq D} I(X; \hat{X}) \text{ bits} \tag{B.20}$$

Transfer Entropy
The transfer entropy $T_{x_{\text{past}} \to y_t}$ is the average information that past values x_{past} of X provide about the current value y_t of Y, over and above the information that y_{past} itself provides about y_t,

$$T_{x_{\text{past}} \to y_t} = I(y_t; y_{\text{past}}, x_{\text{past}}) - I(y_t, y_{\text{past}}) \text{ bits} \tag{B.21}$$

References

[1] Applebaum, D. (2008). *Probability and Information: An Integrated Approach*, Second Edition. Cambridge University Press.

[2] Avery, J. (2012). *Information Theory and Evolution*. World Scientific Publishing.

[3] Baeyer, H. (2005). *Information: The New Language of Science*. Harvard University Press.

[4] Bishop, C. (2006). *Pattern Recognition and Machine Learning*. Springer.

[5] Cover, T. and Thomas, J. (1991). *Elements of Information Theory*. John Wiley and Sons.

[6] Edinburgh, T., Eglen, S., and Ercole, A. (2021). Causality indices for bivariate time series data: A comparative review of performance. *Chaos: An Interdisciplinary Journal of Nonlinear Science*, 31(8):083111.

[7] Ekhlasi, A., Nasrabadi, A., and Mohammadi, M. (2021). Direction of information flow between brain regions in ADHD and healthy children based on EEG by using directed phase transfer entropy. *Cognitive Neurodynamics*, 15(6):975–986.

[8] Feynman, R., Leighton, R., and Sands, M. (1964). *The Feynman Lectures on Physics*. Basic Books.

[9] Fidani, C. (2022). Transfer entropy of West Pacific earthquakes to inner Van Allen belt electron bursts. *Entropy*, 24(3):359.

[10] Friston, K. (2010). The free-energy principle: a unifed brain theory? *Nature Review Neuroscience*, 11(2):127–138.

[11] Gatenby, R. and Frieden, B. (2013). The critical roles of information and nonequilibrium thermodynamics in evolution of living systems. *Bulletin of Mathematical Biology*, 75(4):589–601.

[12] Gibson, J. (2014). Information theory and rate distortion theory for communications and compression. *Synthesis Lectures on Communications*, 6(1):1–127.

[13] Gleick, J. (2012). *The Information: A History, a Theory, a Flood*. Vintage.

[14] Guizzo, E. (2003). The essential message: Claude Shannon and the making of information theory. Available from Massachusetts

Institute of Technology at `http://dspace.mit.edu/bitstream/handle/1721.1/39429/54526133.pdf`.

[15] Hawking, S. (1975). Particle creation by black holes. *Communications in Mathematical Physics*, 43(3):199–220.

[16] Jaynes, E. and Bretthorst, G. (2003). *Probability Theory: The Logic of Science*. Cambridge University Press.

[17] Kathpalia, A. and Nagaraj, N. (2021). Measuring causality. *Resonance*, 26(2):191–210.

[18] Landauer, R. (1961). Irreversibility and heat generation in the computing process. *IBM Journal of Research and Development*, 5:183–191.

[19] Lee, J., Nemati, S., Silva, I., Edwards, B., Butler, J., and Malhotra, A. (2012). Transfer entropy estimation and directional coupling change detection in biomedical time series. *Biomedical Engineering Online*, 11(1):1–17.

[20] MacKay, D. (2003). *Information Theory, Inference, and Learning Algorithms*. Cambridge University Press.

[21] Massey, J. (1990). Causality, feedback and directed information. In *Proceedings of the 1990 International Symposium on Information Theory and its Applications (ISITA-90)*, pp. 303–305.

[22] Mattingly, H., Kamino, K., Machta, B., and Emonet, T. (2021). *Escherichia coli* chemotaxis is information limited. *Nature Physics*, 17(12):1426–1431.

[23] Nemenman, I., Shafee, F., and Bialek, W. (2002). Entropy and inference, revisited. In *Advances in Neural Information Processing Systems 14 (NIPS 2001)*. MIT Press.

[24] Newton, N. (2016). Transfer entropy and directed information in gaussian diffusion processes. *arXiv preprint*, arXiv:1604.01969.

[25] Orange, N. and Abaid, N. (2015). A transfer entropy analysis of leader-follower interactions in flying bats. *The European Physical Journal Special Topics*, 224(17):3279–3293.

[26] Paninski, L. (2003). Estimation of entropy and mutual information. *Neural Computation*, 15(6):1191–1253.

[27] Pierce, J. (1980). *An Introduction to Information Theory: Symbols, Signals And Noise*. Dover.

[28] Reza, F. (1961). *Information Theory*. McGraw-Hill.

[29] Rieke, F., Warland, D., de Ruyter van Steveninck, R., and Bialek, W. (1997). *Spikes: Exploring the Neural Code*. MIT Press.

[30] Ruddell, B. and Kumar, P. (2009). Ecohydrologic process networks: 1. Identification. *Water Resources Research*, 45(3). DOI:10.1029/2008WR007280.

[31] Schreiber, T. (2000). Measuring information transfer. *Physical Review Letters*, 85(2):461.

[32] Seife, C. (2007). *Decoding the Universe: How the New Science of Information Is Explaining Everything in the Cosmos, From Our Brains to Black Holes*. Penguin.

[33] Shannon, C. (1948). A mathematical theory of communication. *Bell System Technical Journal*, 27:379–423.

[34] Shannon, C. (1959). Coding theorems for a discrete source with a fidelity criterion. *Institute of Radio Engineers, International Convention Record*, 4(142–163):1.

[35] Shannon, C. and Weaver, W. (1949). *The Mathematical Theory of Communication*. University of Illinois Press.

[36] Shojaie, A. and Fox, E. (2022). Granger causality: a review and recent advances. *Annual Review of Statistics and Its Application*, 9:289–319.

[37] Stone, J. (2022). *Information Theory: A Tutorial Introduction, Second Edition*. Sebtel Press.

[38] Wallis, K. (2006). A note on the calculation of entropy from histograms. Technical report, University of Warwick, UK.

[39] Wang, Y., Chen, C., and Chen, W. (2022). Nonlinear directed information flow estimation for fNIRS brain network analysis based on the modified multivariate transfer entropy. *Biomedical Signal Processing and Control*, 74:103422.

[40] Wibral, M., Vicente, R., and Lindner, M. (2014). Transfer entropy in neuroscience. In *Directed Information Measures in Neuroscience*, pp. 3–36. Springer.

[41] Zhang, D., Lee, H., Wang, C., Li, B., Pei, Q., Zhang, J., and An, Y. (2011). The causality analysis of climate change and large-scale human crisis. *Proceedings of the National Academy of Sciences*, 108(42):17296–17301.

Index

average, 9, 69

binary
    digit, 3, 5
    digit vs bit, 5
    number, 34, 69
    rate distortion function, 54
binomial coefficient, 32
bit, 3, 7, 20, 69
byte, 37, 69

capacity, 2, 29, 69, 74
channel, 2, 17, 69
channel capacity, 1, 29, 69
codebook, 48, 69
codeword, 69
communication channel, 1
compression   complexity
        causality, 61
conditional
    entropy, 40, 45, 47, 61, 64,
        69
    probability, 69
continuous, 17, 44, 49, 69

decoding, 2, 29, 48
die, 12, 21, 43
difference coding, 35
differential entropy, 20, 49, 69
directed information, 61
discrete, 9, 42, 69
distortion, 52

encoding, 1, 2, 23, 29, 35, 47,
        56, 70
entropy, 9, 70
    conditional, 40, 45, 47, 61,
        64, 69
    definition, 9

differential, 20
    exponential   distribution,
        25
    Gaussian distribution, 26,
        49
    joint, 42, 45, 61, 70
    maximum, 23
    negative, 25
    transfer, 61, 72
    uniform distribution, 23
entropy vs information, 16
equiprobable, 3, 13, 42
equivocation, 47, 52, 70
expected value, 9, 70
exponential distribution, 25

Gallager code, 59
Gaussian
    channel, 49
    distribution, 26, 49, 55, 65
    rate distortion function, 55
Granger causality, 61
gzip, 37

histogram, 17, 35, 70

iid, 9, 34, 49, 52, 70
independence, 9, 34, 46, 49, 70
information, 1, 3, 5, 10, 16, 20,
        29, 51, 63, 70
information theory, 1, 17, 31,
        39, 59, 61
information vs entropy, 16

joint entropy, 42, 45, 61, 70
joint probability, 42, 70

law of large numbers, 32, 70
laws of information, 2

logarithm, 4, 7, 32, 44, 71

Mars Rover, 59
maximum entropy distribution, 23
mean, 20, 25, 26, 71
message, 2, 29, 39, 48, 71
mutual information, 39, 47, 64, 71

nats, 33
noise, 2, 39, 47, 64, 71
noisy channel coding theorem, 2, 47, 53

outcome, 5, 9, 12, 20, 71
outcome value, 12, 24, 30, 71

power, 50
probability
    definition, 71
    density, 19, 23
    density function, 17, 23, 71
    distribution, 9, 12, 25, 42, 71
    joint, 42, 70
    mass function, 71

random variable, 9, 17, 23, 71
rate, 2, 29, 52, 72
rate distortion function, 53, 72, 74
    binary, 54
    Gaussian, 55
rate distortion theory, 51, 72
redundancy, 34, 72
residual uncertainty, 21

Shannon information, 7, 10, 42
Shannon, Claude, 1, 7, 31
signal-to-noise ratio, 50
source, 2, 29, 47, 55
source coding theorem, 2, 9, 29, 31, 37, 51
standard deviation, 26, 72
surprisal, 5, 9, 17, 72

theorem, 72
    noisy channel coding, 2, 47, 53
    source coding, 2, 9, 29, 31, 37, 51
transfer entropy, 61, 72, 74
transmission rate, 31, 51, 72

uncertainty, 2, 16, 20, 40, 47, 51, 61, 72

variance, 26, 50, 55, 72